P9-DEO-869

DISCARDED BY
WELLES-TURNER
MEMORIAL LIBRARY
GLASTONBURY, CT

NASA   NASA   NASA   NASA   NASA

AMERICA in SPACE

NASA   NASA   NASA   NASA   NASA

AMERICA in SPACE

WENDY BAKER

Crescent Books
New York

A QUARTO BOOK

Copyright © 1986 by Quarto Marketing Ltd.

All rights reserved. No part of this publication may
be reproduced, stored in a retrieval system, or
transmitted, in any form or by any means,
electronic, photocopying, recording, or
otherwise, without the prior written permission of
the copyright owner.

1986 edition published by Crescent Books,
distributed by Crown Publishers, Inc.

**Library of Congress Cataloging-in-Publication
Data**
Baker, Wendy.
   NASA: America in space.
   Includes index.
   1. United States. National Aeronautics and Space
Administration. 2. Astronautics—United States.
I. Title.
TL521.312.B345   1986   629.4'0973   85-25731
ISBN 0-517-60364-0

NASA: America in Space
was prepared and produced by
Quarto Marketing Ltd.
15 West 26th Street
New York, New York 10010

Editor: Louise Quayle
Copy Editor: Hilary Sterne
Art Director: Richard Boddy
Layout/Production: Alison Lee, Chris Cancelli
Production Manager: Karen L. Greenberg

All photographs courtesy of NASA

Typeset by I, CLAUDIA Inc.
Color separations by Hong Kong Scanner Craft Company Ltd.
Printed and bound in Hong Kong by Leefung-Asco Printers Ltd.

h g f e d c b

DEDICATION

To the original seven astronauts for their tremendous courage, to the seven members of the *Challenger* crew, Michael J. Smith, Francis R. (Dick) Scobee, Ronald E. McNair, Ellison S. Onizuka, Sharon Christa McAuliffe, Gregory Jarvis, and Judith Resnik, to whom a nation is eternally grateful, to Kent Alexander for his brilliant ideas, and to Dr. Jill Buyon for her valuable support.

ACKNOWLEDGMENTS

Special thanks to Jakki Foster of the NASA photo library for her cooperation on this project.

CONTENTS

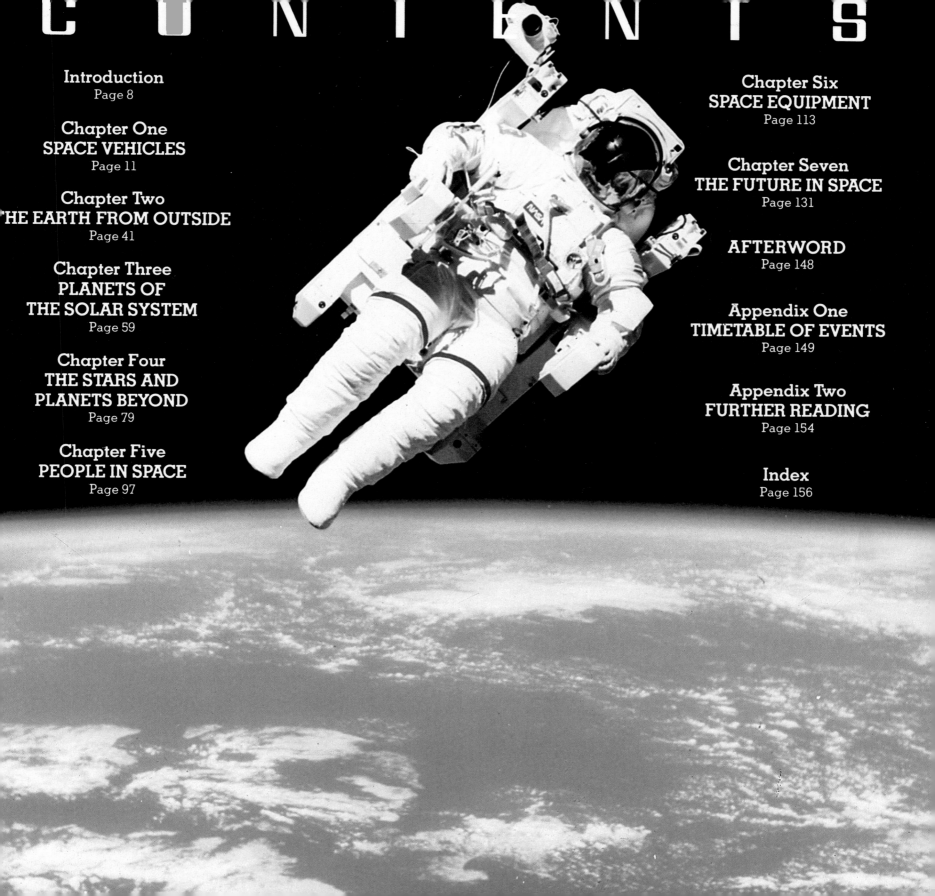

Not more than thirty years ago, space was a vast, uncharted sea full of foreboding mysteries. Very few people dreamed of launching a satellite into the earth's orbit and only the most far-thinking scientists considered exploring other planets. Clearly, space travel was not the foremost consideration of our nation.

Then, on October 4, 1957, the "beep, beep" signal from the Russian satellite *Sputnik 1* was heard around the world. The Soviet Union had orbited the world's first satellite. The American public's response was swift and widespread. Our indisputable certainty that the United States led the world in technology was shattered. Not only had the Russians been first to go into space, but *Sputnik 1* was nearly sixty times bigger than the drawing board satellite of the United States. Our nation was chagrined and the pressure to beat the Russians was growing. The space race was on!

A visual history of NASA is, in many respects, an historical survey of American pride and patriotism. The space program has been fraught with budgetary restrictions and exprimental set-backs, but the overriding theme has been one of "full speed ahead." As we approach the thirtieth anniversary of one of America's most important scientific programs, it is important to consider the steps we have taken to get into space, how we have executed these steps, and what that history implies for the future.

Imagine for a moment that we are back in a time when flight itself, much less spaceflight, is just a dream. Space, in our pretechnological minds, is merely a conceptual mystery, a curiosity to be explored. To Americans it is the new frontier, the new west where space cowboys pursue their wanderlust. As time passes, however, and America moves into the Atomic age of invention and unprecedented technological advances, our images of space begin to change. As space was imagined by the American public in the 1940s and 1950s, the joy and mystery of a new frontier gave way to the Buck Rogers heroics of America's space sol-

dier. With this in mind, our quest into space means much more than pure scientific research. Today, space exploration implies growth for industry, the military, and for average citizens as we seek alternatives for the day when the earth is no longer habitable. Our activities there have far-reaching effects on our lives on earth today and in the future.

NASA: America in Space is a visual account of our nation's journey into the new frontier of outer space. From the very first days of sending monkeys into space to test out the new equipment, to the present days of soliciting applications for the average citizen to board the Space Shuttle, *NASA: America in Space* traces every momentous step of the way. Never before has such a complete pictorial analysis of NASA's activities been assembled. NASA's technological advances are traced with stunning photographs—from the first rockets to the futuristic drawings of a space center. Through the carefully selected photographs in this book, the mysteries of the universe have been captured.

NASA: America in Space is unique in that the history of the space program is presented in a subject by subject format rather than as a chronological account of NASA's activities. "Space Vehicles" illustrates the exciting progression of rocketry; who the men were who first had the vision of sending rockets into space; how the first Mercury-Redstone rocket compares to the orbiting laboratory known as the Space Shuttle; and how the concept of the moon landing was conceived and carried out.

"The Earth from Outside" is a collection of unquestionably some of the most beautiful photographs taken of our planet. After astronaut L. Gordon Cooper radioed to Houston that he could see highways, buildings, and chimney smoke from the Mercury rocket back in 1963, camera shutters have been wide open on all subsequent missions. NASA even went to the extent of launching satellites solely for the purpose of photographing land and sea details. Not only

is the earth seen from a startling new perspective, but vital information is gathered on its precious resources.

"Planets of the Solar System" describes the amazing discoveries of Mars, Venus, Jupiter, and Saturn from NASA's fly-by probes and discloses the future plans for planetary landings and explorations. And "The Stars and Planets Beyond" dares to discuss what we know of extraterrestrial civilizations, in addition to what we are beginning to uncover about galaxies beyond our own.

"People In Space" is a tale of America's heros—of the kind of people it takes to dare to do things no human being has ever accomplished—who are instrumental in the advancement of our civilization. Their story isn't always a happy or optimistic one. It is filled with jealousies and tragedies of everyday life. The myths and realities of these brave adventurers lives is revealed, plus the success story of Dr. Sally K. Ride—America's first female astronaut.

"Space Equipment" illustrates the amazing Manned Maneuvering Unit, the device that allows astronauts to become human satellites; the Hubble Telescope, which can see 14 billion light-years into the past; and Spacelab, the laboratory that carries out a myriad of experiments on the habitability of outer space.

"The Future in Space" is a "must read" for anyone who is curious about the twenty-first century. Space industrialization and manufacturing have already begun. NASA offers "Getaway Specials" to corporations who want to manufacture their products in the optimum, gravity-free environment of space. Venture capitalists are investing, too, in private forays into space. Blueprints for space stations and space colonies are on the drafting boards of aeronautical engineers. It is only a matter of time before space is our next conquered frontier. *NASA: America in Space* is an album of valuable historical events that we will all want to remember before the past gets too far behind, and its portents for the future are forgotten.

chapter one
SPACE
VEHICLES

There is no stronger force in this
world than an idea whose time has come.

Two hundred mile
planet earth, at t
phere, the supe
Challenger soa
17,500 (28,000 km
the flight deck, (
and Mission Spe
make out the cu
through a snowy v
ratory, a team of s
x-ray telescopes a
matter of minutes,
come in, the ten
space comes to a
lenger hurtles h
twenty-five times
time it enters the t
of our atmospher
miles from the e
have lost enough
safely on the space

This may sound
Who, but it is rep
voyage of the Spa
tion System—the
advanced space
are the days of th
cury-Redstone ro
dows, barely enou

*The Mercury Redst
Freedom 7 lifts off t
astronaut Alan B. S
the first United Stat
flight. The spacecr
minutes and 22 sec
of 116 miles, and tr
5,180 miles per hou
demonstrated the a
control of the space
weightless.*

The Space Shuttle lifts away from the launch pad to begin its fifth flight and first operational mission. The Shuttle took off at 7:19 A.M. on November 11, 1982.

Alan B. Shepard, Jr., and was capable of only one fifteen-minute suborbital flight. In comparison, the Space Shuttle is an orbiting laboratory, office, and hotel. It has two levels large enough to accommodate living and working space for seven people, plus an enormous compartment for cargo. With the advent of the Space Shuttle Transportation System, space travel is becoming more routine, more enterprising, and is involving a greater variety of people.

The very term "space vehicle," conceived in science fiction, is only a few decades old. It conjures images of high-tech spacecraft designed in the mode of *Star Trek's Enterprise* that suggest a permanency in space. NASA focuses its missions on voyages of long duration rather than shooting rockets into orbit only to have them return quickly to earth. These tests imply earth-saving missions not unlike those of Flash Gordon; indeed, Gordon's space heroics are not so far off—we are witnessing reality catching up to fantasy.

State-of-the-art space vehicles didn't appear by magic, however. Before NASA existed many tests and experiments were carried out by scientists to see what type of vehicle could take us into space. The original idea of manned rockets traveling beyond the atmosphere grew out of the ideas of what was then a new breed of inventors in the early part of this century: Robert Hutchings Goddard of the United States, Konstantin

The original seven astronauts selected for Project Mercury. Left to right: Malcolm Scott Carpenter, Leroy Gordon Cooper, Jr., John Herschel Glenn, Jr., Virgil Ivan Grissom, Walter Marty Schirra, Jr., Alan Bartless Shepard, Jr., and Donald Kent Slayton.

Eduardovich Tsiolkovsky of Russia, Herman Oberth of Germany, and Robert Esnault-Pelterie of France. They were inspired by science fiction writers Jules Verne and H. G. Wells who dared to discuss space travel in ways that made it sound not only exciting but downright feasible. The four inventors surmised from their theoretical investigations that the rocket, which was already used extensively in warfare at the turn of the century, was the only propulsion system that could operate in the near-vacuum of outer space. Despite their successful experiments, however, they received little support or encouragement from the public who, for the most part, felt humans had no business invading the heavens.

In the decades to follow, public attitude changed little except to acknowledge that aeronautics was necessarily a hobby of the idle rich. Research in aerodynamics was kept on the back burner except when warfare required that money be pumped into technological weapons. World War II for example, spawned an impressive array of new technology created by the massive war effort, including the ballistic missile. These powerful rockets—the Redstone, the Titan, and the Atlas—demanded a new role in postwar United States' technology. Russia had begun her space program and the United States government would not be left behind.

Thus, by the mid-1950s, America's space program was underway. President Eisenhower signed into law the National Aeronautics and Space Act of 1958, and by October of that same year, the National Aeronautics and Space Administration (NASA) was established in an effort to make the United States the leading nation in space sciences.

Immediately NASA went to work on a ten-year plan for space flight that would begin with a manned flight, then an earth-orbital flight, and, finally, circumlunar expeditions. Next, scientific satellites would be launched to measure the features of the near-space environment. Lunar and planetary probes to Mars and Venus would follow along with weather satellites, the final step being the development of large launch vehicles for lifting heavier cargo.

The United States was off! It was a race between the United States and Russia to

John H. Glenn in the Mercury 6 capsule Friendship 7 watches a weightless tube of applesauce during a snack. Glenn was in orbit 4 hours and 55 minutes while the spacecraft made 3 earth revolutions during his first flight.

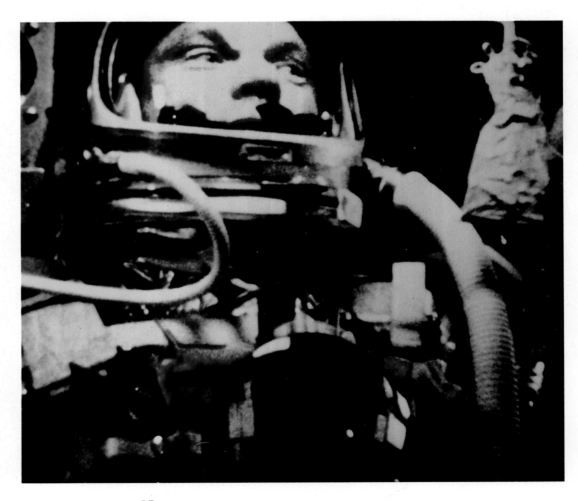

Astronaut John Young, wearing a pressure suit, ejects from his parachute harness after a simulated water landing. This is an integral part of survival training exercises at the Naval Training Tank.

NASA recovery operations in action. Navy frogmen assist Walter M. Schirra, Jr., command pilot of Gemini 6, and astronaut Thomas P. Stafford in opening their hatches. The spacecraft splashed down in the Atlantic on December 16, 1965, after a highly successful 25 hour and 52 minute mission in space. While in space the spacecraft rendezvoused with the Gemini 7.

occupy the solar system. Space was no longer a Buck Rogers fantasy of exploration, it became a territory to control. At issue now was who would dominate the new frontier. If the United States could not afford to build rockets as large as Russia's, then NASA would invest money into putting the first man on the moon.

Project Mercury, a ballistic missile coupled with the Air Force launch vehicle Redstone, was NASA's first rocket designed to put a man in space. It was described as a fully automated system in which the astronaut did not need to turn a hand; in fact the astronaut was considered a redundant component of the vehicle who would be needed only as a repairman or manual conductor if the automated system broke down.

The original astronauts—Alan Shepard, Gus Grissom, John Glenn, Scott Carpenter, Walter Schirra, L. Gordon Cooper, and Donald Slayton—vehemently objected to this concept and argued that they should be able to override the Mercury's automatic system, if only to correct malfunctions. This mission qualified as one of the most dangerous in American history and the astronauts, who were unprecedented heroes, were going to be the first human beings shot into space atop a rocket that no one was sure was foolproof. It was only logical that they would want more control over the vehicle in case anything went wrong, and their demands forced NASA to real-

One of the many chimpanzees specially trained for the Mercury Redstone 2 flights prior to sending men into space. This chimp is shown sitting in the seat in which it will ride during the 16-minute ballistic missile flight. Wires attached to its feet were to give electrical shocks in case the chimp did not perform properly. During the flight, the environmental control and recovery systems were tested. The chimps were trained at the Aeromedical Field Laboratory, Holloman Air Force Base, New Mexico.

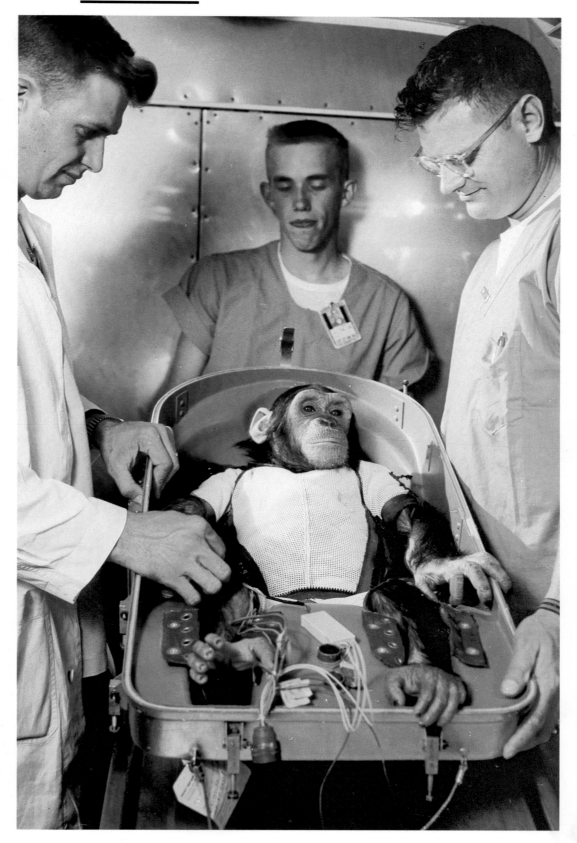

The blast-off of the Mercury-Atlas 6 spacecraft Friendship 7, *taking John Glenn on the first manned orbital flight.*

ize the danger of considering them redundant components.

The building of the first Mercury rocket was already underway, however, and little, if any of it allowed an astronaut much control. Dimensions were kept as tight as possible in order to keep the weight down. Once all the instrument panels, radio hookups, tubes, tanks, and an emergency parachute were crammed inside, the leftover space was just big enough for a human body to squeeze into. Even the astronaut's seat had been sculpted to his back and legs to fit perfectly. Two little portholes were inserted in the capsule on both sides above his head. The only way of seeing the outside world was through a periscope. A window, it was believed, would invite ruptures from the change in atmospheric pressure. By the second Mercury flight, however, the astronauts' demands were met. The new design included a pilot's window and a hatch on the capsule that the astronaut could open himself after landing.

A total of six Mercury spacecraft were launched, beginning May 5, 1961, with the rocket *Mercury 3. Freedom 7,* the rocket's capsule, completed a fifteen-minute and twenty-two-second suborbital flight at an altitude of 116 miles (185.6 km.) in which Astronaut Shepard traveled 297 miles (475.2 km.) and demonstrated his ability to manually control the spacecraft under conditions of weightlessness. At the third blast-off of a Mercury rocket, the *Friendship 7,* the launch vehicle was switched to the heavier, more powerful Atlas D. This massive booster propelled John Glenn through three earth revolutions, making him the first American to orbit the planet. Project Mercury ended on May 15, 1963, after L. Gordon Cooper orbited the earth twenty-two times in a little more than thirty-four hours—about the same time it took Charles Lindbergh to fly from New York to Paris in 1927.

NASA's number one goal in the early sixties was to land a man on the moon and return him safely to earth before the decade was out; however, NASA was not prepared to go directly from Project Mercury to Project Apollo. There had to be a step in between. Hence, Gemini, a new manned spaceflight project, was announced on January 3, 1962.

Gemini's role was to bridge the gap between Mercury and Apollo by solving the questions of space rendezvous and extravehicular activity—the essential components of a successful moon landing. After a set of spacecraft had stabilized in earth orbit, it would then be boosted into the lunar gravitational field. The smaller module of the two craft would then leave the mother craft in lunar orbit and land with its two passengers on the moon. Following lunar reconnaissance, the astronauts would blast off in the top half of the module and rejoin the mother craft in lunar orbit where it would fire up for the return to earth.

Engineers and technicians prepare to evacuate the white room atop the launch vehicle erector. Both hatches are secured on the Gemini 4 *spacecraft by 7:35 A.M. on June 3, 1965. Launch was at 10:16 A.M. with astronauts James A. McDivitt and Edward H. White II onboard. The* Gemini 4 *completed 62 earth revolutions in a flight lasting 97 hours and 56 minutes.*

NASA's Gemini 4 spacecraft lifts off from Launch Complex 19 at Cape Kennedy on June 3, 1965. The launch was delayed by difficulties encountered in lowering the launch vehicle erector tower. The spacecraft was placed into a 100 to 175 statute mile orbit of the Earth.

Astronaut Edward H. White II is shown performing his spectacular space feat during the third orbit of the Gemini-Titan 4 flight. White floats into space, secured to the Gemini 4 by a 25-ft. umbilical line and a 23-ft. tether line, both wrapped together with gold tape to form one cord. White became the first American astronaut to leave his spacecraft while in orbit. He remained outside the spacecraft for 21 minutes. White wears a specially designed space suit and an emergency oxygen supply chest pack for his extravehicular activity. He is holding a hand-held Self Maneuvering Unit which he used to move about in the weightless environment. White and command pilot, James A. McDivitt, performed other scientific and engineering experiments before completing their 62-revolution mission.

Gemini had the same design as the Mercury capsule, except that this time the interior was enlarged to hold a crew of two. The launch vehicle was the Air Force's Titan II, a missile with enough thrust to put the weightier Gemini into earth orbit. By 1965 Gemini was considered man-rated. One of the program's objectives was to orbit men in space for at least the seven days it would take Apollo to go to the moon, land, and return.

Gemini 4 remained in orbit for four days and Edward H. White was the first astronaut to space walk. With no specific tasks to perform, White gleefully floated about taking dozens of photographs. He was attached to Gemini by an eight-meter (roughly eight-yard) umbilical cord and held a gas gun for maneuvering. The experience was exhilarating, and White could have wafted indefinitely if mission control had not commanded him to return to the capsule after nearly thirty minutes of being lost in space.

Gemini explored many more avenues of spaceflight than was originally intended and proved to be a technological learning experience. *Gemini 7* completed 206 earth revolutions in a little

This multiple exposure photograph was the result of eleven separate exposures on one sheet of film when the Gemini 10 *spacecraft was rocketed into orbit from Cape Kennedy on July 18, 1966. The fan effect of the gantry being lowered and the Titan launch vehicle lifting off was achieved by making ten exposures through a mask and slit that worked on a pivot. The mask covered the entire film area except for the slit that exposed only the gantry as it went down. This mask was then removed and replaced with a fan-shaped mask that blocked out the gantry area with the final exposure showing the lift-off. This marked the eighth manned flight in NASA's Gemini program.*

The Apollo 11 *Lunar Module photographed from the command service module during rendezvous in lunar orbit. Here the module is making its docking approach to the command module. The large dark-colored area in the background is Smith's Sea on the lunar surface. The earth rises above the lunar horizon.*

over 330 hours and rendezvoused in orbit with *Gemini 6* one foot away. *Gemini 8* achieved the first docking between a manned spacecraft and an unmanned space vehicle, the *Agena. Gemini 11* set a new altitude record of 850 miles (1,360 km.). On the final Gemini flight, astronaut Edwin E. Aldrin, Jr., worked outside the spacecraft for a record five hours and thirty minutes.

Throughout Gemini's operational period, Apollo was plugging away toward its completed stage. The first rocket of the project, *Apollo 7,* was launched on October 11, 1968. A Saturn 1B launch vehicle put the three astronauts into earth orbit for eleven days, where they tested the command module. All systems were go. On October 21, 1968, *Apollo 8* passed out of one gravitational field of the solar system and into another. *Apollo 10* (May 18–26, 1969) was the full-dress rehearsal of the moon landing minus the descent to the lunar surface. It was successful. On July 16, 1969, *Apollo 11* lifted off for the ultimate mission. Four days later the lunar module separated and de-

Astronaut Edwin E. Aldrin, Jr., deploys the Passive Seismic Experiments Package on the lunar surface. Apollo 11 *astronauts Neil A. Armstrong, Michael Collins, and Aldrin were launched to the moon by a Saturn V launch vehicle on July 16, 1969. Armstrong and Aldrin actually landed on the moon while Collins circled the moon in the command module.*

Apollo 11 *propels itself away from the launch tower on July 16, 1969, on its way to becoming man's first lunar landing mission. Astronauts Neil A. Armstrong, Michael Collins, and Edwin E. Aldrin, Jr., fulfilled the goal set by President Kennedy on May 25, 1961 to put a man on the moon before the end of the 1960s. After separating from Command Service Module* Columbia *in lunar orbit, Armstrong and Aldrin landed on the Sea of Tranquility on July 20th in the Lunar Module* Eagle.

View of the Apollo Command Module with astronaut Michael Collins aboard as seen from the lunar module. Astronauts Neil Armstrong and Edwin Aldrin in the lunar module have separated from Apollo 11 and prepare to go to the lunar surface. The terrain in the background is of the far side of the moon.

scended to the lunar surface. After a manually controlled, cliff-hanger landing with only a few seconds of fuel remaining, Neil Armstrong announced in a controlled yet excited tone, "Houston …Tranquility Base here…the *Eagle* has landed."

Several hours later, millions of television viewers a quarter million miles away watched Armstrong set foot on the lunar surface and heard the immortal words: "One small step for man; one giant leap for mankind." The ten-year national commitment had been fulfilled. Edwin E. Aldrin, Jr., joined Armstrong and together they bounded around on the grey, powdery surface collecting samples of lunar rocks, while astronaut Michael Collins circled the moon in the *Columbia* command module.

Apollo 12 ventured to another moon site—the ghostly Ocean of Storms— where an unmanned spacecraft, the *Surveyor 3,* had been squatting for two and a half years. Astronauts Charles Conrad and Alan L. Bean removed pieces from the spacecraft, including a television camera, to analyze them after thirty-months exposure to the lunar environment. *Apollo 15* brought along the lunar rover, an electric-powered, four-wheel-drive vehicle. In this lunar buggy astronauts David R. Scott and James B. Irwin roamed the moon's landscape, visiting a number of unearthly landmarks. *Apollo 17,* the seventh and last lunar landing,

Astronaut John W. Young, commander of the Apollo 16 *lunar landing mission, leaps from the lunar surface as he salutes the United States flag at the Descartes landing site during the first* Apollo 16 *extravehicular expedition. Astronaut Charles M. Duke, Jr., lunar module pilot, took this picture. The Lunar Module* Orion *is on the left with the Lunar Rover parked beside it. The shade behind Young is from the lunar module. Stone Mountain dominates the background.*

Here Alan B. Shepard, Jr. (foreground) and Edgar D. Mitchell work through experiments on the first extravehicular activity of their Apollo 14 mission. Mitchell is working at the deployment site of the Apollo Lunar Surface Experiments Package. Note the checklist attached to Shepard's left wrist.

Astronaut Eugene A. Cernan riding in the Lunar Rover during the first Apollo 17 extravehicular excursion to the Taurus Littrow landing site. The mountain in the background is the east end of South Massif. This view of the stripped-down rover is prior to load-up. Equipment later loaded onto the rover included the ground-controlled television assembly, the lunar communications relay unit, the high-gain antenna, the low-gain antenna, lunar tools, and other scientific equipment.

Scientist-astronaut Owen K. Garriott, Skylab 3 science pilot, is performing extravehicular activity at the Apollo Telescope Mount of the Skylab space station cluster in earth orbit. Garriott has just deployed the Skylab Particle Collection Experiment. The experiment is mounted on one of the solar panels and its purpose is to collect material from interplanetary dust particles to study their impact phenomena.

Astronaut Jack R. Lousma, Skylab 3 pilot, participates in the August 6, 1973 extravehicular experiment in which he and Owen K. Garriott deployed the twin pole solar shield to assist in shading the Orbiter 1 workshop. The reflection of the earth in Lousma's helmet visor has a surreal effect.

proved to be the most productive scientifically. Its expedition to the Taurus-Littrow site, where both the oldest and the youngest moon rocks can be found, concluded the Apollo moon-landing project, which lasted eleven-and-a-half years, cost $123.5 billion, and put twelve men on the moon.

The next manned spaceflight program was Skylab, the first American-manned space station. It was born in the period of enthusiasm for manned spaceflight during the race to the moon in the 1960s. At that time NASA was anticipating an era when space exploration would blossom into a number one priority supported by large fiscal budgets. The major objective of Skylab was to determine if people could physically withstand extended stays in space and continue to work.

Other Skylab mission objectives were to evaluate techniques designed to gather information on the earth's resources and to conduct a major investigation of the sun using Skylab's special solar telescopes.

Skylab was built from the S-1VB stage of a Saturn V moon rocket. The Saturn's hydrogen tank was converted into a spacious two-story accommodation for a three-man crew. Skylab was the first space vehicle to offer creature comforts. It had 13,000 cubic feet (364 m.³) of space; water for showers and other needs; facilities for heating meals; five freezers; and lockers that stored soap, towels, and changes of clothing. But because of financial cutbacks, Skylab had to be trimmed back to one orbital workshop and three astronaut flights.

Each of these missions included medical and industrial experiments and solar observations from which a vast amount of data was collected. During the flight of *Skylab 4* the astronauts observed and photographed comet Kohoutek as it rounded the sun. One astronaut, who spent long hours at the solar observatory, witnessed the shooting orange lava of a solar flare—the first one to be recorded from beginning to end. A solar flare results from gigantic energies released in the destruction of magnetic fields that arc above the solar surface. Perhaps the most significant knowledge gathered from Skylab, however, was that people can survive in space without physiological problems and that some industrial processes have their greatest potential in space.

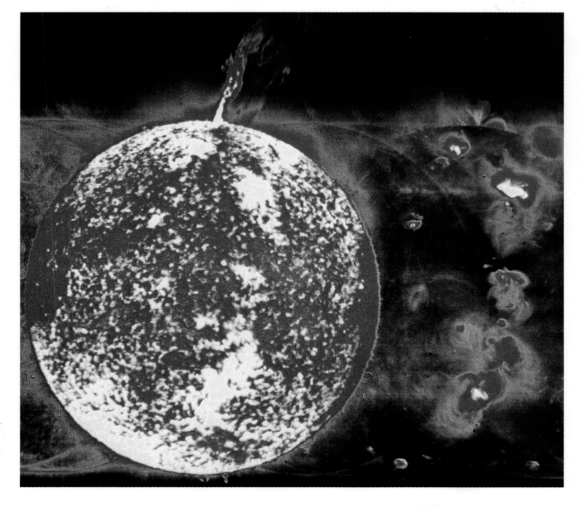

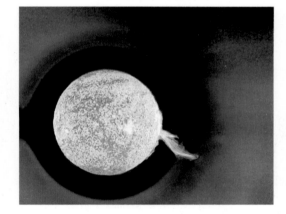

Skylab provided much new solar data that was made possible by its solar telescope. The images here were originally black and white. Color enhancement of the images for data reduction was a new technique that grew out of the Skylab missions. Solar Prominences are shown in action (left) in this ultraviolet image of the sun. A Colossal Coronal Transient Balloon (above) dwarfs the disk of the sun and the surge in the chromosphere that started it. The eruptive prominence lashes out like a tongue of fire and propells the great disturbance. The ultraviolet image of the sun is superposed for clarity.

Astronaut Donald D. Slayton and Cosmonaut Aleksey A. Leonov in Orbital Module. The two crews of the 1975 joint United States-Soviet Apollo-Soyuz Test Project (ASTP) docking in earth orbit were astronaut Thomas P. Stafford, commander, astronaut Vance D. Brand, command module pilot, and astronaut Slayton, docking module pilot, of the American crew; Cosmonaut Leonov, commander, and Cosmonaut Valeriy N. Kubasov, engineer, of the Soviet crew.

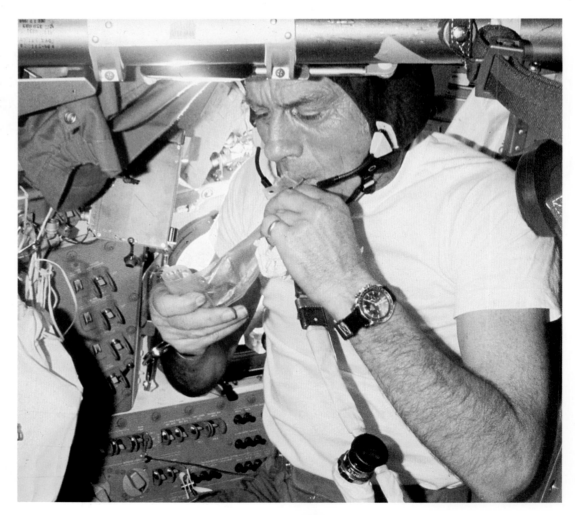

Astronaut Slayton takes a break for a snack during the ASTP, history's first cooperative international manned space flight. After six years of joint discussions, negotiation, and working group sessions that took place in both the United States and the Soviet Union, the mission proved a huge success. The jointly designed docking module that made the link-up possible was an important piece of space hardware developed for the mission.

A mission of an entirely different nature occurred on July 17, 1975, when an Apollo spacecraft joined a Soviet Soyuz in orbit 140 miles (224 km.) above the earth. The Apollo-Soyuz Test Project, as it was called, was history's first international manned spaceflight. It was the result of six years of joint decisions and negotiations that took place in both countries. The mission produced one unique piece of hardware—the jointly designed docking module which made the linkup possible. The three United States astronauts—Tom Stafford, Donald "Deke" Slayton, and Vance Brand—and the two cosmonauts—Aleksey Leonov and Valerey Kubasov—shared meals, exchanged gifts, and conducted a series of scientific experiments. This was the first step toward a cooperative, international space program.

The next step may be a space rescue demonstration in which the two nations would maneuver spacecraft close together and trade astronauts, proving that one nation could, if necessary, rescue the marooned space crew of another. This idea was proposed by the United States and Moscow has agreed to it, paving the way, perhaps, for a joint mission to the moon or Mars.

In addition to the Apollo-Soyuz Test Project, NASA was planning other innovative spaceflights in the 1970s. What is now thought of as the most advanced flying machine ever made, the Space Shuttle Transportation System, was conceived by NASA and approved by President Nixon in the early 1970s. From that point forward it consumed nearly all of NASA's attention. The goal for the Space Shuttle was to replace all of the current

Astronaut Thomas P. Stafford (foreground) and astronaut Vance D. Brand in the Apollo Command Module. Millions of television viewers worldwide watched as three astronauts and two cosmonauts shared meals, exchanged gifts, and conducted a series of significant scientific experiments during the Apollo-Soyuz Test Project on July 17, 1975.

The hazy light of dawn illuminates the Space Shuttle Columbia *as it arrives at Launch Pad 39A following a six-hour move from the Vehicle Assembly Building. This is the second roll-out for the STS-9 vehicle after replacement of a nozzle on the aft segment of the solid rocket booster that forced officials to delay the Spacelab 1 launch. This mission was the first to last as long as nine days and had six crew members including the first European to fly aboard a United States spacecraft.*

and expendable launch vehicles and serve as a reusable transport to space for the development of commercial operations and the construction of a permanent space station: Of the Shuttle's three main elements, a space plane, called the Orbiter, two rocket boosters, and an external tank, only the tank needs to be replaced in every mission. One way to think of it, then, is as a space truck that delivers its cargo, such as the Spacelab, or domestic or foreign satellites, and then returns for a new mission.

The first Orbiter, called the *Enterprise* at the request of *Star Trek* fans, made its initial test voyage on August 12, 1977, with the help of a Boeing *747*. The Boeing, acting as the mother plane, took the Orbiter up on its back and released it at an elevation of 22,800 feet (6,949 m.). This flight and subsequent others revealed problems with the engine and the heat-shielding tiles that protect the airframe when the Orbiter reenters the atmosphere; consequently, the project was delayed while NASA worked to determine the causes and correct these malfunctions.

On April 12, 1981, the project resumed when the Space Shuttle *Columbia* made its debut and successfully completed a two-day orbital test flight. After completing three more test flights, it was ready for its first operational use. Finally, the days of expensive, expendable space vehicles were over.

There are now four major orbiters: *Columbia, Challenger, Discovery,* and *Atlantis.* Each one is about the size of a DC-9 commercial airliner—122.2 feet

Technicians prepare to hoist Spacelab 1 *out of its test stand and into the payload transport cannister at Kennedy Space Center. This transfer was a milestone in the processing of this pressurized module and its attached pallet. The module was built by the European Space Agency and flew aboard the Space Shuttle Orbiter* Columbia *on the STS-9 mission.*

The first operational flight of the Space Transportation System begins on schedule at 7:10 A.M. on November 11, 1982, as the STS-5 mission begins with a smooth lift-off from Launch Pad 39A. Aboard the Columbia is the first four man crew ever to fly in a single space launch, and the first commercial satellite payload for the Space Shuttle program.

The fourth Space Shuttle begins to take shape as its external tank is "mated" or attached to twin solid rocker boosters inside. During the launch, the Orbiter's main engines ignite and gulp down propellants from the mammoth tank, while the boosters begin firing to provide the lion's share of the tremendous lift-off thrust.

The payloads for the 41-D Space Shuttle flight are shown loaded in Discovery's cargo bay. With the Orbiter in the vertical position at Pad A, the payloads are from top to bottom, OAST-1, SBS-D, Telstar S-C, and Syncom IV-2. The six crew members are Commander Henry W. Hartsfield, Jr., Pilot Michael L. Coats, Mission Specialists Judith A. Resnik, Steven Hawley, Richard Mullane, and Payload Specialist Charles D. Walker.

(37.25 m.) long with a delta-shaped wing 78.06 feet (23.79 m.) across, and a tall, vertical fin and rudder with movable flaps to serve as speed brakes.

Inside the Orbiter is the forward fuselage, which is divided into two levels. The upper level is the flight deck where a crew of seven are stationed at control panels. In the forefront of the flight deck is a cockpit where the pilot and mission commander sit. The lower level, or mid-deck, is the living area for the astronauts, where they eat, sleep, and wash. Behind the mid-deck is the cargo bay—an enormous compartment measuring sixty feet (19.29m.) long and fifteen feet (4.57 m.) wide. It can carry cargo weighing up to thirty tons (27.21 metric tons). Astronauts must don spacesuits before entering this area because unlike the front fuselage, it is not pressurized.

Below the cargo bay are several liquid hydrogen and oxygen tanks that supply the fuel for the on-board electrical power system. In the tail of the Orbiter are clustered three main engines, which also burn liquid oxygen and hydrogen, and the twin engines of the Orbital Maneuvering System (OMS) that propel the Orbiter into earth orbit and slow it down to reenter the atmosphere.

The Orbiter itself is mounted on the side of a huge external tank to which are strapped two Solid Rocket Boosters. The boosters, 149.16 feet (45.46 m.) tall and 12.14 feet (3.7 m.) in diameter, and the external tank, 154.2 feet (47 m.) tall and 27.56 feet (8.4 m.) in diameter, dwarf the Orbiter.

The flights are launched from the Ken-

Space art—"The Right Stuff on Final"—an oil painting by artist William S. Phillips realistically depicts the Space Shuttle Columbia and Chase 1 during the final moments before touchdown at Dryden Flight Research Center, California, on April 14, 1981. This was the first landing of the Columbia.

The crawler-transporter, spanning the two lanes of the turnpike-wide "crawlerway," moves the fourth Space Shuttle to Launch Pad 39A. Traveling at a top speed of one mile per hour, the crawler made the three-and-a-half mile journey in just under six hours—a fast trip for a vehicle carrying an 11.7 million pound load.

"Launch of the Columbia STS-1," a mixed-media painting by artist Chet Jezierski portrays an unusual view of the Space Shuttle Columbia as it is launched into space for its historic maiden two-day long voyage on April 12, 1981.

Columbia *rests in the transfer aisle of the Vehicle Assembly Building as preparations are made to hoist it into High Bay 3 for mating with the solid rocket boosters and external tank. It was towed from the Orbiter Processing Facility before dawn, backed out of the building at 3:54 A.M. and rolled into the V.A.B. about 25 minutes later to complete the latest segment of its second journey to the launch pad.*

nedy Space Center in Cape Canaveral, Florida. The current launching schedule is one per month eventually increasing to one every two weeks. At the space center, the Shuttles use the same two launch complexes that the Apollo rockets used to start their journeys to the moon. The Shuttle arrives at the launch complex mounted vertically on the mobile launch platform on the back of a giant crawler transporter that positions the complete unit over the blast pit. The vehicle is supported on the launch platform by four attachments on the solid rocket boosters. At the base of the platform are boxlike fueling stations that are pumped aboard the external tank in the last hours before lift-off.

At lift-off, the Orbiter's liquid-fuel engines fire in concert with the rocket boosters. After clearing the tower, the Shuttle accelerates to the speed of sound, and within seconds is out of sight. Minutes later, the Solid Rocket Boosters' fuel is exhausted and the rockets are blasted free from the external tank. After they have descended to a three-mile (4.8 km.) altitude, their nose caps spring off and parachutes open to slow their descent into the ocean. Waiting ships tow them back to the launch center.

The Shuttle, continuing to gather speed and height, now consists of the Orbiter and the external tank. At an altitude of seventy-five miles (120 km.), the external tank, nearly on empty, separates from the Orbiter. What is left of it after reentering the atmosphere falls into the Indian Ocean and is not recovered.

The Orbiter's main engines cut off and

Suspended over a recaptured communications satellite, astronauts Dale A. Gardner (left) and Joseph P. Allen IV (right) make light of the status of the stranded satellite. Though their pose is in good fun, it hints, perhaps, at the future for private industry and investment in space activities whether they be deploying communications satellites like this one or investing in space manufacturing endeavors.

NASA placed in earth orbit the first spacecraft designed specifically for the study of solar flares. The mission represents a major step toward a better understanding of the violent nature of the sun and its effects on earth. The Solar Maximum Mission spacecraft was launched from Cape Canaveral, Florida on February 14, 1980 by a Delta Rocket.

All eyes are on President Reagan as he and Columbia astronauts Commander Thomas K. Mattingly and Pilot Henry W. Hartsfield celebrate the fourth return of the space ship at Dryden Flight Research Facility, Edwards Air Force Base, California. Behind them is the Space Shuttle Enterprise, used for Shuttle approach and landing tests. The more than half million visitors who attended this Fourth of July event also saw the Challenger take off attached to its 747 carrier aircraft.

Pictured here is the seventh launch of the Space Shuttle in June of 1983. This mission was highlighted by the first direct landing from space by an Orbiter to the Shuttle Landing Facility. During the mission the crew deployed Indonesian and Canadian satellites and used the remote manipulator system to deploy and retrieve a platform for space experiments called the Shuttle Pallet Satellite.

it coasts along until firing the twin OMS engines. Speed is boosted to 17,500 miles (28,000 km.) per hour. It reaches an altitude of 150 to 200 miles (240 to 320 km.) and begins a continuous orbit around the earth. One orbit takes one-and-a-half hours.

At the end of its mission, the Orbiter must brake to below orbital velocity so the earth's gravity can capture it. It then turns around so it is traveling tail first, fires the OMS rockets against the direction of the flight, and descends as a glider. This last phase is the most difficult part of the flight. The Orbiter is the heaviest such glider ever built, weighing 150,000 pounds (67,950 kg.), and when it enters the outer fringes of the atmosphere it is traveling twenty-five times the speed of sound. Slowly it loses speed and begins to rotate. At 1,700 feet (518.16 m.) the Orbiter's nose tilts up and it begins to descend at an angle seven times sharper

than that of an airplane. At 900 feet (274.32 m.), the landing gears extend. Fifteen seconds later it lands horizontally on a three-mile (4.8 km.) runway at Kennedy Space Center.

The Space Shuttle Transportation System introduced a new phase in the United States space program. *Columbia* and her sister ships will provide economical and routine access to space and give the United States a permanent presence in space. Exciting possibilities in scientific exploration and industrial operations will open up possibilities that, if realized, may one day help to solve the world's problems and benefit mankind. And thanks to the Space Shuttle, one day we may all have the opportunity to take part in this endeavor. Today we routinely watch the space launches on television; tomorrow anyone who is able to fly in an airplane will be able to board the Space Shuttle and ride into orbit.

Space Shuttle Challenger *prepares to touch down on runway 15 at Edwards Air Force Base, completing the seventh mission of the Space Transportation System. The mission was scheduled to land at Kennedy Space Center, but was diverted to the dry lake bed in California when fog settled in at Cape Canaveral. Commander Robert Crippen made a perfect landing following the rigorous seven-day mission. The mission is notable for carrying the first five-member crew, including the first woman astronaut, Dr. Sally K. Ride.*

chapter two
THE EARTH FROM OUTSIDE

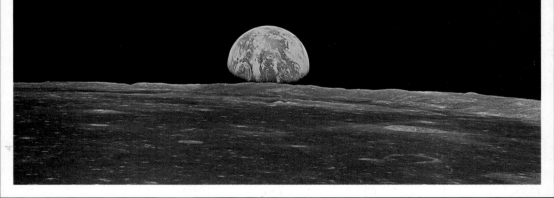

We shall not cease from exploration
And the end of all our exploring
Will be to arrive where we started
And know the place for the first time.

—T. S. Eliot

On their way to the first landing on the moon, Apollo 11 astronauts took this photograph of a storm over the sea west of Australia. The clouds in this vast panorama look as though they had been smoothed over by a trowel. This broken strata formation is typical over the Pacific.

(Previous page) This view of the rising earth—240,000 statue miles away—greeted the Apollo 11 astronauts as they came from behind the moon after the lunar orbit.

THE EARTH FROM OUTSIDE

"This is Mercury to Houston...this is Mercury to Houston, come in please."

"This is Houston, Mercury. What's the trouble?"

"You're not going to believe this," said Major Cooper, "but I can actually see highways."

"*Highways*? Cooper, that's impossible—you're a hundred and fifty miles up in space."

"I know it sounds crazy, Houston, but it's the truth. Heck, I can even make out buildings and chimney smoke."

There was a long pause, then, "Gordon, are you feeling okay?"

"I've never felt better."

"Even so, I think we'll put you under observation for a few days, run some tests on you."

"Whatever you say, Chief. But I'm telling it just like it is. Over and out."

And so it began. Like a ballerina dancing alone in an empty theater, the earth has been revolving in the darkness of space unobserved for 5 billion years. Then in 1963, during the longest flight of the Mercury rocket, in which the *Faith 7* circled the earth twenty-two times, astronaut L. Gordon Cooper caught a startling glimpse of the earth from space. In the years to follow, the earth would become the focus of unprecedented observation.

The next time around, the Gemini as-

tronauts went into orbit fully prepared, bringing cameras and rolls of color film. NASA scientists pored over their photographs as though they were souvenirs from a once-in-a-lifetime vacation. As they compared pictures of Los Angeles that had been shot only six months apart, scientists spotted very subtle changes in the landscape due to erosion. When Texas crops gradually began to unfurl after the end of a dangerous drought, Gemini cameras showed red—the infrared film's color response to vegetation. In Arizona snow was discovered on top of the mountains; in Louisiana flood damage was recorded after a major storm. NASA quickly realized the potential in observing the intricate details of the earth's surface—it was like looking at the planet under a giant microscope. They then began working on the initial stages of the Earth Resources Technology Satellites (ERTS) that would scan every part of the earth down to the last detail.

After the Gemini voyages, NASA was aiming for the moon but not without a

One month after its volcanic eruption, NASA took this picture of Mount Saint Helens (left). Extensive ice and rock debris in the foreground are the result of the blast that blew out 1,300 feet of the mountain and the north wall of the summit crater. This view taken from the northwest, looking up the north fork of the Toutle River, was photographed by a NASA Ames Research Center U-2 aircraft flying at 60,000 feet.

This photograph (below) shows 13,000 square miles (34,000 km²) of southern California, including Los Angeles (lower right) and other cities of the Los Angeles Basin and San Fernando Valley. The light-colored triangular area in the upper right quarter of the scene is the Mojave Desert, bounded on the southwest by the San Andreas fault and on the northwest by the Garlock fault. The Mojave is separated from the Pacific Ocean in this area by the mountains that make up the Transverse Range. The southern San Joaquin Valley is in the upper left, marked by the checkerboard pattern of farming areas.

The earth as seen from the Apollo 17 spacecraft (right). A star background has been added by an artist.

This view of hurricane Kamysi in the Indian Ocean is by far the best that has been provided by manned spaceflight, (below). Astronauts told ground control they could actually see waves through the storm's eye. The eye's location was east of the northern tip of Madagascar.

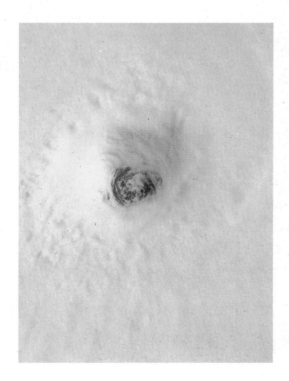

backward glance at the earth. Apollo astronauts were awestruck by the sight of the earth shrinking into a small blue ball as they raced off into space; and as they rounded the moon, rising before them was a brilliant sphere against the blackness of space. Partly visible through the swirling clouds were Asia and Africa where—240,00 miles (384,000 km.) away—millions of people were going about their lives. It was the first time that anyone had seen the earth in its entirety and fully realized what it was that they called home base.

The earth, viewed in cosmic perspective, is a galactic afterthought—an insignificant mote of dust in the starlight. Its mass is only three-millionths that of the sun, which is itself one of the lesser stars of the billions of stars in the billion galaxies that can be seen only with the most technologically advanced telescopes. Yet our planet is the only one known to us where water exists in a liquid state and which supports life. That water can remain liquid and life can continue on earth is due to the fact that it is the right distance from the sun to maintain the proper temperature range.

The earth's geography is unique, too.

This is the first full scene produced on Landsat 4 showing a terrain sparse in vegetation dominated by landforms and other geologic features. The location: Death Valley, California/Nevada. Most major landmarks are physiographic, including the Panamint Range, the Grapevine, Funeral, and Black Mountains, Spring Mountains, Las Vegas Valley, Searles Lake, the Granite and Avawatz Mountains in the northern Mojave Desert. The false-color rendition of the scene shows most of the ranges to be largely barren. The distinctive red, indicating forests, appears on the Spring Mountains and central Panamints.

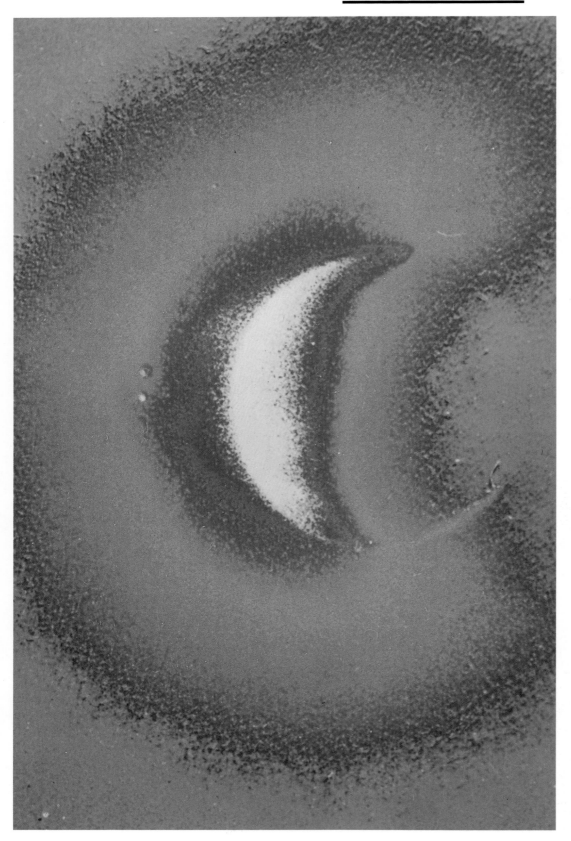

A color enhancement of a photograph of earth exposed in far ultraviolet light by the Apollo 16 UV camera, (left). Commander John W. Young took the photo on the mission's first extravehicular activity. The halo of low density hydrogen which surrounds earth—called the geocorona—appears as the crescent in the center. The spike at lower right is auroral activity over the south magnetic pole. The light that produced this photo, from which this artificially reproduced view was made, was about one-third the wavelength of the most blue light visible to the naked eye.

This is a color composite photo of the Finger Lakes Region of New York taken from the NASA Earth Resources Technology Satellite (ERTS-1) at an altitude of 568 statute miles (914 km.), (below right). Three colors—green, red and infrared—were recorded separately by the satellite and combined at NASA's Goddard Space Flight Center. Bright red indicates healthy crops, trees, and other green plants that reflect infrared. Some of the notable landmarks are Lake Ontario (upper left), Rochester, N.Y. (far left center), Syracuse, N.Y. (far right center), and the Finger Lakes (bottom half of image).

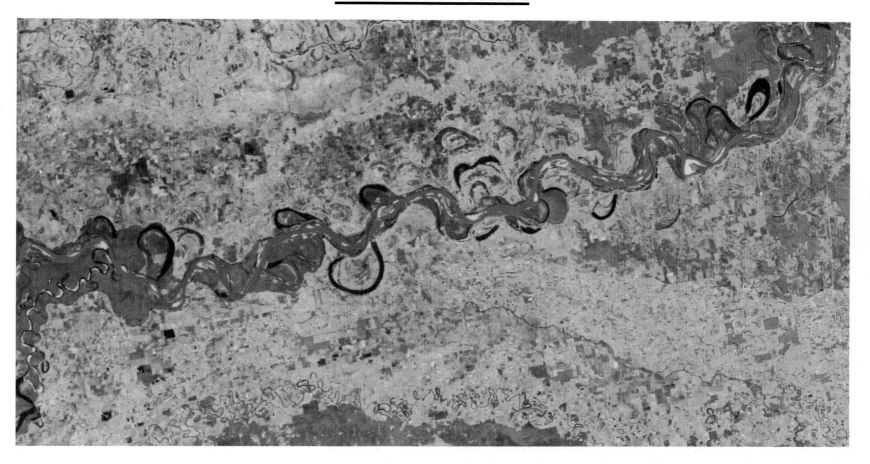

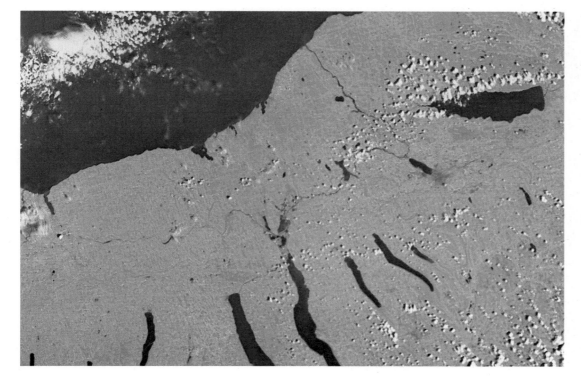

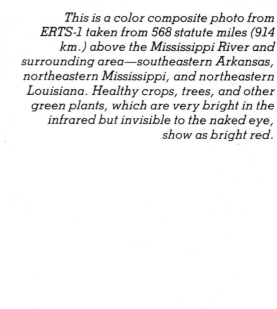

This is a color composite photo from ERTS-1 taken from 568 statute miles (914 km.) above the Mississippi River and surrounding area—southeastern Arkansas, northeastern Mississippi, and northeastern Louisiana. Healthy crops, trees, and other green plants, which are very bright in the infrared but invisible to the naked eye, show as bright red.

With the exception of Venus, the other planets are merely globes of ice and gas or inactive lumps of rock that will remain unchanged for hundreds of millions of years.

But there are disadvantages to the earth's changing topography—erosion and destruction. The earth's natural resources are limited and easily exhausted; her environment can be irreversibly polluted and her animal and plant life erased forever. To cope with the problems posed by the deterioration of natural resources, we need a total view of the earth in order to understand it. Only from space is it possible to simultaneously collect global data on the conditions of the atmosphere and oceans, agriculture and geography.

NASA launched its first Earth Re-sources Technology Satellite, later re-named *Landsat 1,* in 1972. Since then, unmanned Landsat satellites have been in orbit continuously. Flying at an altitude of 500 miles (800 km.)—nearly three times that of the Shuttle—to keep in orbit with the sun, they are able to observe the entire planet with the exception of small areas near the North and South Poles. The satellites are designed to orbit in such a way that they can maneuver directly over nearly every point on the earth's surface. All of the photographs are taken from this vantage and look just like a map: flat, two-dimensional, and with the top pointing north.

The special cameras that are employed are adapted from those used in World War II spy planes. They have multi-spectral sensors each of which

Another view of the New York/New Jersey area, taken from ERTS-1, (below). Some of the notable geographical landmarks are the Hudson River (upper left down to middle right); New York City and Staten Island (middle right); Long Island (upper right to middle right); Newark, Jersey City, and Elizabeth, N. J. (middle right); and Connecticut (upper left). Federal agencies participating with NASA in this project are the Departments of Agriculture, Commerce, Interior, and Defense, and the Environmental Protection Agency.

This ERTS-1 photo of the New York/New Jersey area shows how heavily developed this small spit of land is, (facing page). The metropolitan area is surrounded by red areas that indicate the vegetation in New Jersey. Pale blue shows the urbanized areas of the Jersey shore and city burroughs while brownish-green shows Manhattan's high density urban development; white shows concrete areas and blue/black is water.

In this late summer scene of Boston, Massachusetts, the trees and fields appear their natural green, (right). The lakes appear dark, but water in Boston Bay is a deep blue, with streaks of greenish-blue representing sediments and other effluents. Central metropolitan Boston shows white mixed with dark spots, which indicates high levels of light reflection from building materials. Near the Charles River (left to right) is the downtown section where a small green rectangle denotes the Boston Common.

This Landsat image shows Mt. Kilimanjaro, that at a height of 19,340 feet (5894 meters), is the highest point in Africa, (below). An immense volcanic pile measuring 50 miles across (80 km.), Mt. Kilimanjaro has three eruptive centers: Shira, Kibo, and Manwensi. The volcanoes were thought to be dormant, but vigorous fumarolic activity was discovered in 1933. In this scene an immense range of geologic conditions can be seen, from the Hyiri Desert of southern Kenya to the glaciers of Kibo. This image shows the great influence elevation has on precipitation in East Africa—the higher the mountain, the greater the vegetation.

scans a different part of the color spectrum: one sensor views the world in green wavelengths, one in red, and two in infrared. Each sensor identifies the features on the earth's surface by the energy they emit. Rocks, soil, and vegetation each have a different color identification. Data from the green sensor appear blue; red appear green; and infrared appear red. In Landsat images, shades of orange or red represent trees, plants, or healthy crops while cities and industrial areas appear dark grey. Light pink indicates suburbia, water is shown by various shades of blue, and barren land is light grey.

The advantages of such a sophisticated system have been demonstrated in various ways: Landsat imagery has corrected the scaling on maps of South America and Africa; it has identified minerals and oil deposits in what was thought to be barren land and pinpointed potentially productive areas in the tropics; and, by checking the moisture content of soil, Landsat has helped scientists to determine the best time to plant and harvest crops. In a matter of hours it can inventory the different plants of an entire continent and special Landsat satellites are even investigating the longterm effects of heavy industrial pollution on cities.

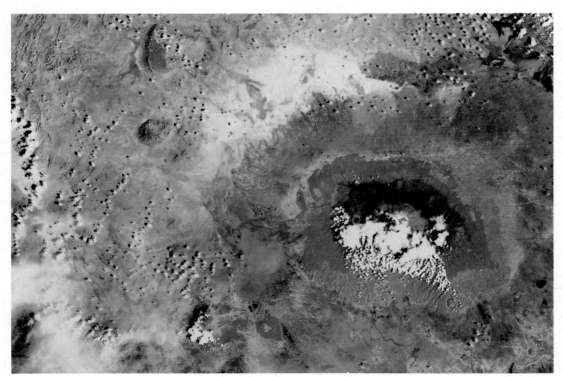

The area shown lies in the eastern San Luis Valley of southern Colorado, (facing page). The town of Alamosa is just off the bottom left edge of the image. Part of the Great Sand Dunes National Monument is visible below the right center edge. The blue area represents snow on the Sangre de Crestos Range. Yellows and browns indicate generally barren, rocky terrain. A number of circular fields (plowed that way) are also green indicating active crops.

The sun fades into an eclipse behind the black disc of the earth as the Apollo 12 astronauts—Conrad, Bean, and Gordon—head for the second lunar landing mission, (right).

Landsat 4 *captured this scene of Des Moines in 1982, (below). To the north of the city is a man-made reservoir. This is one of a series of flood-control dams along the Des Moines River. Interstate 80 can be seen clearly running through the city in an east-west direction. Des Moines and its suburbs appear blue-grey.*

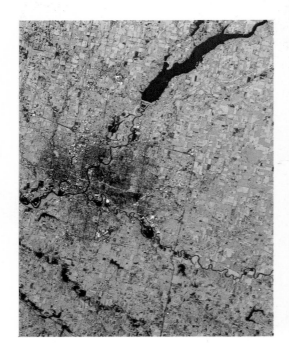

THE EARTH FROM OUTSIDE

Landsat shows remarkable details in and around the metropolitan Washington, D.C. area, (right). Individual government buildings in downtown Washington stand out because their whitish colors are expressed as strong reflections. The shapes of the larger buildings are usually evident. The grass in the playing field of Kennedy Stadium is sharply defined and the runways at National Airport also stand out.

A typhoon in the south central Pacific Ocean, southeast of New Zealand, was photographed during the Skylab 4 mission, (below). The crew was Gerald P. Carr, mission commander; Dr. Edward G. Gibson, science pilot; and William R. Pogue, pilot.

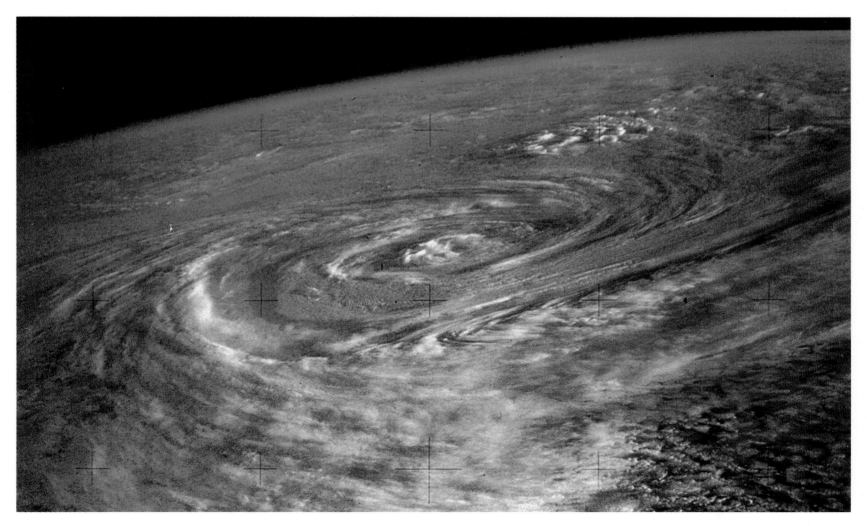

Far from the urban smokestacks and tangled threads of highways, where fleets of icebergs drift in cold and lonely splendor and enormous schools of fish swarm the sea, is another special satellite called Seasat. This NASA invention travels almost 500 miles (800 km.) higher than the clouds and, to date, has made fourteen revolutions of the earth. Devoted exclusively to surveying the world's oceans, Seasat witnesses the birth of hurricanes, cyclones, and typhoons and gives advance warning of their approach to coastal communities. It forecasts ice hazards to shippers, and records fish abundance for the Department of Fisheries and Wildlife. Seasat has thus far given us more information about the earth's waterways than any ocean vessel is capable of, but because of financial cutbacks it has been cancelled.

The Space Shuttle program, on the other hand, is traveling full speed ahead. Every mission has a program of earth observations that have been preselected weeks before take-off. They are chosen based on the time of year, time of the launch, and any unusual weather conditions. The astronauts are alerted by a computer as to when they are nearing their targets so they can be ready to pho-

The Namib Desert is an extremely dry region due to the influence of the cool Benguela current, which flows northward along the coast of Namibia. The area shown here is just north of Luderitz. The dominant physical features are the great sand dunes of the Namib Desert. These dunes are much more complex than they may appear at first glance, and it is difficult to say just what wind directions they imply. The dominant dune types are longitudinal dunes that are considered to form roughly parallel to the prevailing wind. This area has considerable mineral wealth in the form of alluvial diamonds.

The island of Bora-Bora in the Tahiti-Archipelago region is in the center of this photograph, (right). Between the island and the coral barrier reef is an encircling lagoon. As the island sinks, the coral reef grows and will eventually leave a remnant called an atoll. At lower right are the coral-encircled islands of Raiatea and Tahaa. To the upper left is Tapai.

This color composite taken from Landsat 1 shows Northern Niger with the Marzuq Basin to the north and the Tibesti Mountains to the northeast, (below). Also visible is the Mangueni Plateau, a deeply dissected area of gently dipping Paleozoic and Mesozoic sedimentary rock, including the Nubian sandstone. Two major types of geologic features are evident here. The most conspicuous is the family of sand dunes, sheets, and streaks extending from upper right to lower left. The length and parallelism of these features demonstrates the strength and persistence of the regional wind pattern. The second type of feature is the intricate dendritic network of canyons eroded in the plateaus. Much of this erosion must date from the Pleistocene Epoch, when North Africa was much wetter, as present rain levels could not have caused it.

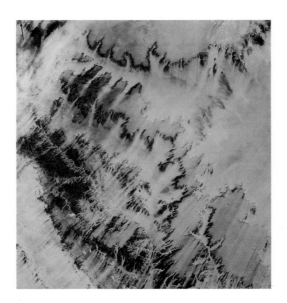

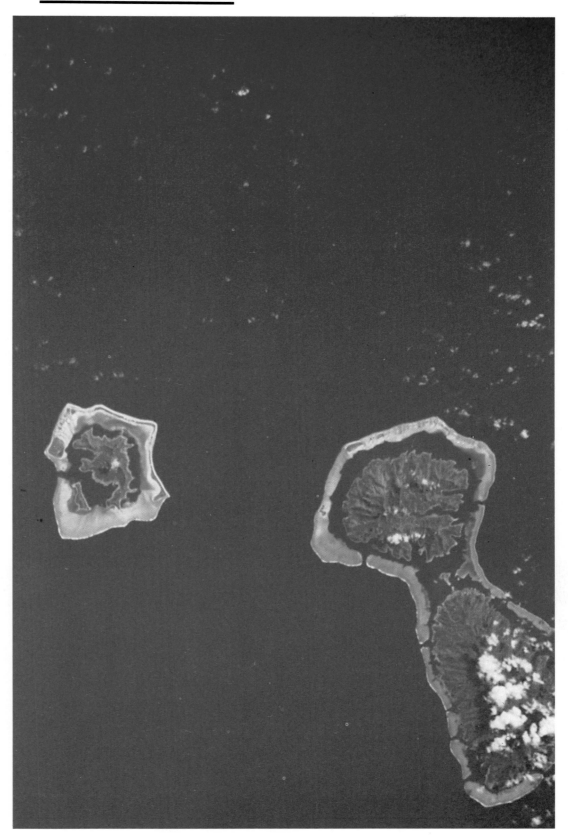

This image was obtained by the multispectral scanner onboard Landsat 2, (right). A part of southwestern Oklahoma appears in the right half of the image. The left half lies within the eastern section of the Texas Panhandle east of Amarillo. The sharp bends of the Canadian River are seen at the top. The Red River, forming the border between Oklahoma and Texas, appears just above the bottom edge. This region falls within one of the major belts of winter wheat grown in the southern Great Plains. Many of the lightly colored squares correspond to farms where this wheat is being cultivated. The southern part of the Anadarko Basin underlies the terrain in this region. This basin contains some of the oldest oil and gas producing fields in the United States.

This Landsat image of the San Francisco Bay Area is a fine example of how the overcast sky hugs the coastline while the land is essentially cloudless, (right). The clouds follow the coastline so uniformly that even the indentation created by Monterey Bay may be seen in the image (lower left center). The Santa Cruz Mountains form a barrier along the peninsula leading down from San Francisco. The detail shown in this picture is tremendously valuable. The agricultural development of the San Joaquin Valley, for example, separated from the bay area by the Diablo range (in the upper right hand portion of the scene) will be valuable to application disciplines that study California's agriculture.

This color composite photograph using red, infrared, and green filters was taken of Colorado by Landsat 1. *Pictured in the landscape are the Rocky Mountain Regional Park, Denver, and Boulder, Colorado.*

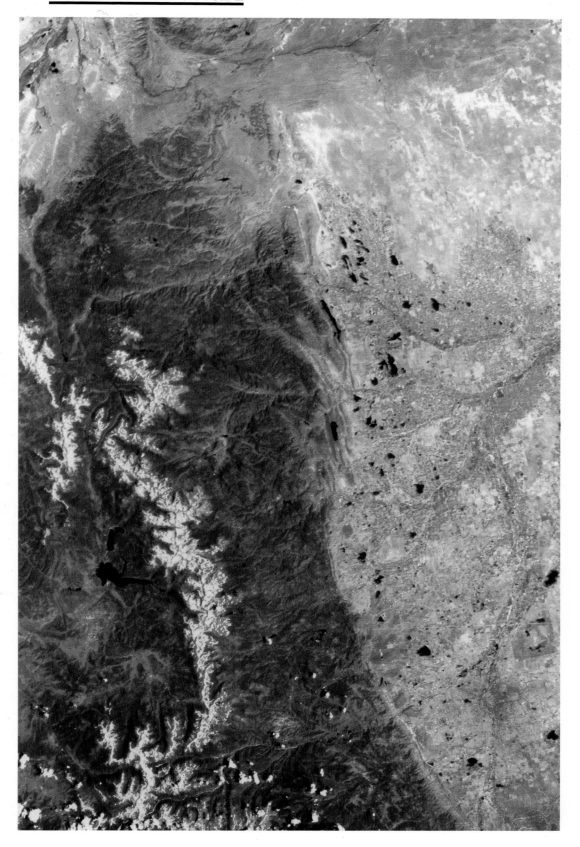

tograph erupting volcanoes, bizarre cloud formations, or patterns of tidal waves. Shuttle photographs do not require interpretation—they are taken with standard cameras using panchromatic film.

Ventures into space will continue to give us vital data about the earth as well as some of the most beautiful photographs of our planet. It is important to add that many spacecraft launched into orbit are put there for the sole purpose of observing the work of our political enemies. The information that they provide is just as valuable to the earth's survival as any other. In the event of a nuclear attack, millions of tons of sooty black smoke from fires would block out the sun, causing sudden and perhaps long-lasting declines in the amount of heat and light reaching the earth. Crops would perish and the people who survived the explosion would face death by starvation. Because we now know how fragile our planet is, and that, thus far, it is the only home we have in the universe, the surveillance these craft provide is necessary to maintain a safe, healthy and peaceful planet.

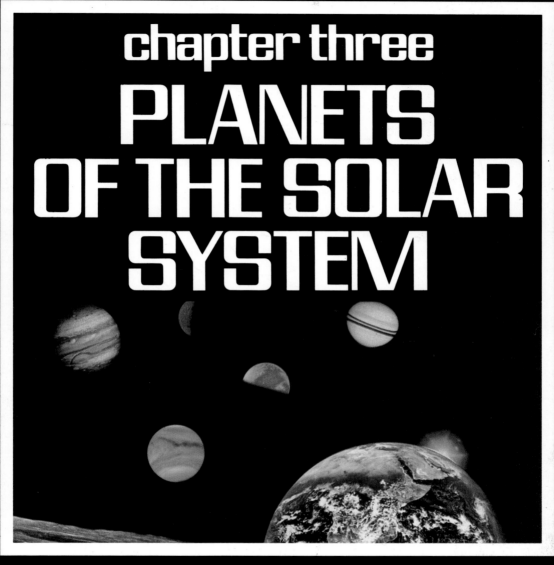

chapter three
PLANETS OF THE SOLAR SYSTEM

Man can learn nothing unless he
proceeds from the known to the unknown.

—Claude Bernard

(Previous page) This montage of the planets in our solar system was created from pictures taken from NASA spacecraft. The terrain in the foreground is of the moon with the earth rising behind it. Directly above the moon is Venus, and the planets Jupiter, Mercury, Mars, and Saturn are shown from top left to right.

PLANETS OF THE SOLAR SYSTEM

Standing before them is a cold, red desert—an empty tract of land, strewn with graveled rocks and, farther ahead, huge volcanic mountains three times higher than Mount Everest.

Captain Bartholomew adjusts his oxygen regulator to the thin Martian atmosphere and motions for the others to follow him out of the Interorbital Transportation System. First steps Dr. Tsiolkovsky, the great-grandson of the Russian rocket inventor. He, too, adjusts his oxygen regulator to the environment. Next follows Dr. Rahman from India and then comes Mission Specialist Marie Tisseret from France. She closes and locks the module door behind her.

"Adjust your regulators to N-7," orders Bartholomew.

"Captain, isn't that too low?" asks Dr. Rahman.

"Not at all," answers Tsiolkovsky. "The air may be thin, but it is hardly dangerous."

They stand four abreast, gazing at the landscape and the hazy pink sky. About a mile (1.6 km.) to the left is an enormous reservoir of frozen water. Mars is covered with these reservoirs, and it is believed that if the ice were to thaw, water hundreds of feet (several kilometers) deep would cover the planet. The crew wants to examine the chemical deposits locked into the ice for clues to the history of the sun. They climb into the Mars Rover and head for the reservoir.

This scene is only imaginary but by the twenty-first century voyages to Mars may well be a reality. Later voyages in this scenario might explore the 2800-mile canyon system, three times deeper and seven times longer than the Grand Canyon. It is expected to contain the entire geological history of Mars.

Up to now, only an unmanned spacecraft, the *Viking 1*, has actually landed on Mars. Touching down on July 20,

This photo of Mars was taken July 26, 1976—the day after Viking 1's successful landing on the planet, (facing page). Local time is noon and the view is southeast from the spacecraft. Orange-red materials cover most of the surface, apparently forming a thin veneer over darker bedrock that is exposed in patches (see lower right). The reddish material may be limonite (hydrated ferric oxide). Such weathering products form on earth in the presence of water and an oxidizing atmosphere. The sky, too, has a reddish cast, perhaps due to scattering and reflection from the reddish sediment suspended in the lower atmosphere.

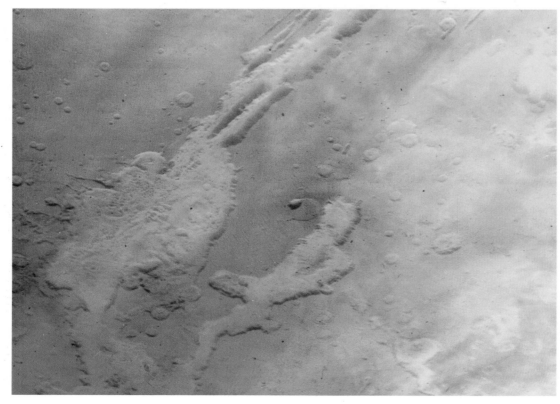

This is a computer-generated false-color exaggeration of the different hues on Mars, (above). Computerized image processing methods such as this separate and amplify extremely subtle color differences among various types of clouds, atmospheric haze, surface frosts, and rock materials. The violet background represents black space and the Martian nightshade. Bright materials, atmospheric haze, surface frost, and bright desert are represented by turquoise, white, and yellow. Dark material on the surface is represented by deep reds and blues. The Martian volcanoes are dark red. A broad band of atmospheric haze (bluish white) extends across the volcanoes.

From 19,200 miles (31,000 km.) above Mars, Valles Marineris—the Grand Canyon of Mars—was photographed by Viking 1, (left). The canyon lies just a few degrees south of the equator and parallels it for 3,100 miles (5,000 km.) east to west. The area covered in this picture is a little larger than Alaska.

1976, it represented the end result of seven years of intense effort at NASA. Prior to Viking, fly-by probes and photographs shot by *Mariners 6, 7,* and *9* were as close as we'd come to the red planet. Of all the other planets in our solar system, Mars, it is believed, holds the greatest potential for supporting life—past or present. Other than the earth, it has the best environment to sustain life in the solar system. It is the only planet with a surface temperature comparable—although significantly colder—than earth's.

Speculation about Mars, which can be viewed as a kind of "halfway world," in part like the earth and in part like the moon, is great. Scientists are immensely curious about how the great rifts and huge volcanoes formed, what caused its climate changes, and whether the whole planet is really lifeless. In 1990, NASA expects to launch the *Mars Observer,* an unmanned spacecraft that will do global mapping of Mars for a full Martian year, which is equal to roughly two earth years.

In the future, Mars will have first priority in any manned solar system exploration because its atmosphere, accessible surface, probable availability of water, and relatively moderate temperatures make it a more suitable environment for humans than that of other planets. Moreover, the resources of Mars include materials that could be adapted to support

The view of Mars from the Viking spacecraft on its approach.

This Martian sunset over the area called Chryse Planitia was photographed on August 20, 1976, by Viking 1, (above). The camera began scanning the scene about four minutes after the sun dipped below the horizon. The Martian surface appears black, and the most prominent feature in the foreground is a silhouette of the top of one of Viking's power system covers (far right). The sky color grades from blue to red looking to the left of the sinking sun.

This color variation is explained by a combination of scattering and absorption of sunlight by atmospheric particles. Scattering by micron-sized particles enchances the blue in the region close to the sun's position. At the larger scattering angles, absorption of blue light by the particles gives the sky a redder tinge.

Shown here is a model of the Mariner spacecraft that was launched on its journey to Mars in May 1971. At the bottom of the photo is the scan platform, carrying two television cameras and other scientific experiments, (left). The green dish is an antenna. The louvers in the body of the spacecraft are for temperature control. The white shroud at the top of the spacecraft is a temperature control blanket for the 300-pound thrust retro-engine. Altogether the spacecraft weighs 2,200 pounds.

human life: the air, an environment that could grow food, and materials that could be converted to fuels, fertilizers, and building materials. If these steps are taken, travel to Mars may be commonplace before the middle of the next century. The first explorers probably will not become permanent residents; rather, they will set the stage for others who want to live and work in this exciting new world.

Venus is the closest planet on our solar side, but its environment is very different from our own. The surface temperature of the planet reaches 900 degrees Fahrenheit (482.2 degrees Celcius) because solar energy gets trapped beneath the atmosphere, causing what is known as a greenhouse effect. The atmosphere is so dense that it bears down on the surface of the planet with a pressure ninety times greater than the atmospheric pressure of the earth—the feeling would be akin to that of being 3,000 feet (914.4 m.) deep in the ocean. Carl Sagan speculates that any organism that could possibly live in so dense an atmosphere would have to have leathery skin and stubby wings with which to fly with little effort.

Venus also has a cloud cover that is twenty miles (32 km.) thick. It is not composed of water droplets like the earth's clouds, but of highly corrosive sulfuric acid which colors it yellowish white. Because of this deep cloud cover and the dense atmosphere, little sunlight reaches the surface of the planet. High noon on Venus would not be any brighter than twilight on earth. The sun would appear as a diffuse red blob, and the sky would be a deep red fog similar to our sunsets.

No one has seen the surface of Venus because it is camouflaged by the toxic clouds. Radar has been able to penetrate the shroud, however, to reveal a relatively flat topography, although there are some craters and one immense volcano.

The first successful fly-by probe of Venus was accomplished in 1962 by the *Mariner 2* after traveling 109 days to reach the planet. Subsequent Mariner missions also investigated Venus, and in 1978 the *Pioneer-Venus 1* and *2* were launched to orbit the planet. The satellites will spend eight years taking pictures, evaluating atmospheric samples, and making radar measurements of the planet's surface.

This is the first image of Venus's northern hemisphere, taken by the Infrared Radiometer aboard the Pioneer-Venus spacecraft in December of 1978. The center white cross indicates the position of the North Pole. The partial coverage seen in this polar view shows us a dark, cool, cloud band near the pole. The temperature is measured to –30 Celsius.

En route to Mercury, Mariner 10's television cameras took this photo of Venus from 450,000 miles away (760,000 km.). The picture was taken in invisible ultraviolet light. The blue appearance of the planet does not represent its true color; it is the result of darkroom processing of the image with a blue filter to enhance the ultraviolet markings on the planet's clouds. The predominant swirl in the photo is at the South Pole.

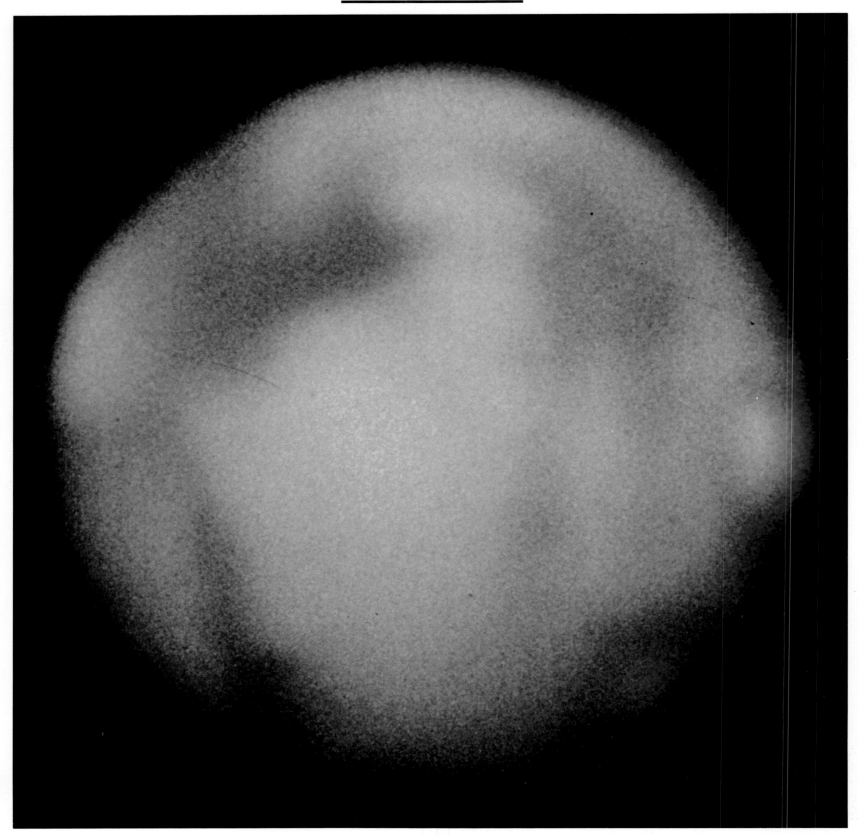

This photograph of Mars during its 1967 opposition was taken for NASA by the Lunar and Planetary Laboratory at the University of Arizona. The white spot at the tip of the image is the North Polar Cap. The other white markings are clouds of haze.

Mercury sits so close to the sun that its rotation has almost been halted. Consequently, Mercury's days are longer than its years. Having a bad day on Mercury would take on immense proportions! Fortunately, because conditions are so inhospitable, there is little chance any of us will live there in the near future. Mercury receives the full range of high-energy radiation emitted by the sun, including extremely damaging x-rays and ultraviolet light. On the sunlit equator the temperature reaches 260 degrees Fahrenheit (126.67 degrees Celsius). On the planet's night side the temperature drops to -270 degrees (-167.78 degrees Celsius). A trip from one side to the other makes the temperature difference between Siberia and the Caribbean seem slight by comparison.

Mercury is too small to retain an atmosphere and so has nothing with which to shield itself from the harsh conditions of space. This is evidenced by its terrain, which is pockmarked with thousands of craters from the bombardment of meteorites. Its sprawling plains are due, in part, to the impact of the meteorites and to volcanic activity.

Mariner 10 left the earth in 1973, and after observing Venus in 1974, it was deflected into an orbit around the sun in which it approached Mercury every six months. From the first three fly-bys, we received streams of data. Soon after, Mercury burned up the fuel that would have prevented it from tumbling, and no further messages were received. Without fuel to stabilize it, the on-board antenna cannot be aimed at the earth to send signals or receive commands.

The granddaddy of all the planets, Jupiter, is two and a half times the combined mass of all the other planets in the solar system. If it were a bit larger it could have been a star generating its own light. Together with its four moons, Io, Ganymede, Callisto, and Europa, Jupiter forms a system that resembles that of the sun and Mercury, Venus, Earth and Mars.

Venus' crescent is shown here in a photograph taken in ultraviolet light by the Pioneer Venus Orbiter in 1978. This image is based on raw spacecraft data without computer enhancement. The dark markings in the equatorial and middle latitude regions are thought to be caused by absorbant cloud material. The clouds are located beneath a veil of haze, which partially blocks the view of the lower atmosphere.

This montage of images prepared from Voyager 1 *photographs gives us a realistic look at the Jovian system, (left). Visible are Jupiter with its four moons: Io, the smallest; Europa (closest to Jupiter); Ganymede (bottom left); and Callisto (righthand corner). A star background was added by the artist.*

Because of its size and the light it emits, astronomers have been aware of Jupiter for four centuries. Few present-day astronomers imagined that it held many surprises until NASA launched *Voyagers 1* and *2* in the late summer of 1977. The most complex robotic intelligence ever built, the Voyagers were designed solely to explore Jupiter. One year after *Voyager 1* blasted off, it began taking amazing photographs of Jupiter from 31 million miles (49.6 million km.) away.

Jupiter is a planet of whirling eddies and violent storms, the largest of which is 16,000 miles (25,600 km.) wide—it could cover three earths. Called the Great Red Spot, this tempest has been raging for over three hundred years. The outer edge of the Great Red Spot, as observed by Voyager, makes a complete counter-clockwise circle once every six days while the center remains motionless.

A ring system, similar to that of Saturn's, was also observed by Voyager. It consists of extremely fine particles of dust about twenty miles (32 km.) wide. The dust particles extend in toward Jupiter to the top of the atmospheric clouds. The outer edge of the ring is hard like the edge of a piece of cardboard.

On Jupiter's moon, Io, eight volcanoes erupted while Voyager was snapping pictures. This was the first ongoing volcanic activity anyone knew of outside of the earth. Voyager also detected a strange, tube-like flow of electricity between Jupiter and Io.

Voyager 1 *took this photo of Jupiter and its two satellites, Io (left) and Europa, (right). Io is about 220,000 miles (350,000 km.) above Jupiter's Great Red Spot. Europa is nearly 375,000 miles (600,000 km.) above Jupiter's clouds. Although both satellites are of equal brightness, they have different colors. Io is a mottled dark orange with dark reddish poles. Its surface composition is unknown, but scientists believe it may be a composition of salts and sulfur. Europa is a lighter shade. In this photo, Jupiter is about 12.4 million miles (20 million km.) away from the spacecraft. There is evidence of circular motion in Jupiter's atmosphere—dominant large-scale motions are east to west, with small-scale movement between the bands.*

Jupiter's Great Red Spot, just emerging from the brief five-hour Jovian night, (right). The Spot is a counter-clockwise rotating storm system that has been raging for 300 years. The outer edge makes a complete circle once every six days while the center remains motionless. It is only one of many storms on Jupiter. One of three bright, oval clouds, which were observed to form approximately forty years ago, can be seen immediately below the Red Spot. This view of Jupiter was obtained by Voyager 1 on February 22, 1979, from a distance of 7.6 million miles (12.2 million km.).

This montage was prepared from images taken by Voyager 1 *during its flight through the Saturnian system in November 1980. Saturn and five of the planet's known satellites are featured. Moving clockwise from right, Tethys and pockmarked Mimas are in front of the planet; Enceladus is in front of the rings; Dione, left forefront; and Rhea off the left edge of the rings.*

After the surprising discoveries made at Jupiter, scientists were reluctant to speculate on what Voyager would find at Saturn. Clearly the most beautiful planet in our solar system with its smooth, amber-banded surface and halo of rings, Saturn is also a great mystery. Earth-based observations draw a sketchy picture of Saturn because it is such a great distance away and telescopic viewing is necessarily limited.

The day before *Voyager 1* swept by Saturn, it flew within 2,500 miles (4,000 km.) of Saturn's largest natural satellite,

Titan, and passed behind it. Titan is shrouded in a thick haze, but infrared instruments and spacecraft radio were able to probe the atmosphere to measure its thickness, temperature, and composition, which proved to be a combination of nitrogen, methane, hydrogen cyanide, and other organic compounds. If it weren't for Titan's low temperature of −288 degrees Fahrenheit, life could thrive on this satellite. Nitrogen is one of the primary components of living matter, while methane could possibly play the same role on Titan as water does on

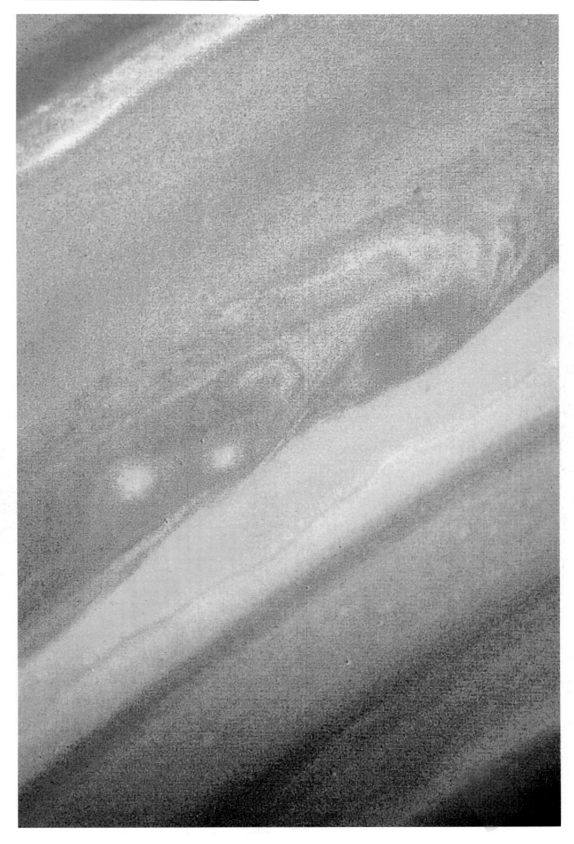

This false-color picture of Saturn's northern hemisphere was assembled from ultraviolet, violet and green filters. The several weather patterns that are evident include three spots flowing westward at about 33 miles per hour. The ribbon-like feature to the north marks a high-speed jet stream where wind speeds approach 330 m.p.h. (150 meters per second). Voyager 2 took this image on August 19, 1981, 4.4 million miles away.

earth—clouds might rain or snow methane, filling rivers and lakes. Hydrogen cyanide is an essential molecule in the building of life-sustaining amino acids.

As *Voyager 1* approached Saturn, it detected that it is visibly flat at the poles due to rapid rotation. Radio emissions from the planet determined the length of Saturn's days to be 10 hours, 39 minutes, and 24 seconds. Saturn receives only one-fourth of the sunlight that reaches Jupiter. Its temperature is thought to be –270 degrees Fahrenheit (–167.78 degrees Celsius).

Winds blow at extremely high speeds on Saturn—Voyager measured winds near the equator of 1,100 miles (1760 km.) per hour. The atmosphere is dense and consists mainly of hydrogen and helium. Scientists have yet to determine what solid surface, if any, exists below the atmosphere. For the most part, they observed swirling cloud patterns, bands of clouds that alternated from bright to dark, and high-speed jet streams. Saturn's clouds are mostly frozen crystals of ammonia ice.

The origin of Saturn's rings is obscure. They are subtle compared to Jupiter's bright rings, possibly because of the clouds formed due to the colder climate. They could have condensed into their present form, or they may be made of de-

bris resulting from the break-up of a satellite. Their composition is not known with any certainty; however, infrared spectra show marks of water ice, indicating the rings could be composed principally of icebergs and/or snowballs ranging from a centimeter to several meters in radius that change daily. The variations are caused by gravitational attractions of nearby satellites that pull millions of particles outward into motion across the rings like ocean waves. Other variations may be due to a pair of tiny satellites—called shepherding satellites—that continuously circle the rings.

The slightly different colors of Saturn's three main rings indicate variations in chemical composition and particle size. As Voyager approached Saturn's rings, more details appeared. The middle ring—referred to as B-ring—has spokes that radiate over a distance of 6200 miles (9920 km.) and are composed of tiny particles. The outermost ring—the F-ring— is composed of three strands, two of which are braided. The braiding occurs when the inner of the two shepherding satellites comes close to the ring. It never looks the same because the satellites and the ring are constantly moving.

This highly enchanced color view of Saturn's ring system was assembled from clear, orange, and ultraviolet frames obtained August 17, 1981, from Voyager 2, (left). Possible variations in chemical composition from one part of Saturn's ring system to another are visible. In addition to the previously known blue color of the C-ring and Cassini Division, the photo shows additional color differences between the inner B-ring and outer region (where the spokes form) and between these and the A-ring.

Voyager 2 captured this view of Saturn and its ring system on August 11, 1981, when the spacecraft was 8.6 million miles (13.9 million km.) away and approaching the large, gaseous planet at about 1 million kilometers a day, (left). The ring system's shadow is cast directly in the equatorial region. Storm clouds in the mid-latitudes are apparent. The ribbon-like feature in the white band marks a high-speed jet stream; there, the westerly wind speeds are about 330 miles per hour.

Saturn as seen from the Voyager spacecraft. A star background was added by the artist, (above).

A montage of images composing the Saturnian System, (facing page).

Besides zeroing in on the rings, Voyager's cameras photographed and measured all the satellites of Saturn, bringing the total number to twenty. Saturn's satellites are different from those that orbit other planets as they are composed of thirty-to-forty percent ice. Enceladus, for example, is almost pure water ice. It is the most reflective body in the entire solar system.

Thirty thousand pictures later, the Voyagers completed their photographic missions. *Voyager 1* has completely finished planetary explorations and is now searching for the boundary of the solar system, where the solar wind fades away and cosmic rays and the wind from other stars replace it. *Voyager 2* is on course for two more planetary close encounters before it, too, heads for interstellar space. In 1986, *Voyager 2* will be within range of Uranus—1.78 billion miles (2.85 billion km.) from the sun—and will start close-up observations of that planet. It will then head for Neptune—2.8 billion miles (4.48 billion km.) from the sun. Observations of Neptune will take place

Neptune and its largest moon, Triton, as visualized by an artist, (right).

*An artist's concept of the planet Uranus
and its rings.*

in the summer of 1989—twelve years after Voyager 2 left the earth. Both spacecraft will be approaching the edge of the solar system by 1990, where, it is hoped, they will report on the transition between the sun's sphere of influence and the vast interstellar space beyond before disappearing forever.

Pluto is the lonely outpost at the edge of our solar system. The sun from this planet would look like nothing more than a brilliant point. Pluto is so far away that other planets—even Neptune, which is closest—would be barely visible. Pluto revolves around the sun only four times in a millenium. It continually eludes the probing of even the most powerful earth-based telescopes; we can only assume that Pluto and its satellite Charon are two huge icebergs. Because of the tremendous distance and cost that would be involved there are no plans, as yet, for even fly-by probes of Pluto.

The exploration of the solar system will stand forever as the great technological achievement of our time. In the past twenty years, men have walked on the moon, robot spacecraft have landed on Mars, and orbital and fly-by probes have encountered each of the planets up to and including Saturn. At long last we are beginning to know other planets as we know earth and to feel at home in the universe.

Pluto and its moon, Charon, in an artist's conception.

chapter four
THE STARS AND PLANETS BEYOND

The Earth is the cradle of mankind,
but one cannot live in the cradle forever.

—K. E. Tsiolkovsky

Pioneer 10, *launched March 3, 1972, is humankind's first attempt to communicate with extraterrestrial civilizations, (above). After approaching Jupiter in late 1973, the spacecraft accelerated with Jupiter's gravity and became the first man-made object to leave the solar system. The spacecraft will take about 80,000 years to travel to the nearest star, about 4.3 light-years away.*

(Previous page) Pictured is Ring Nebula NGC 7293 in a photograph taken by the United States Navy Observatory.

THE STARS AND PLANETS BEYOND

For every human being on earth, there may be 100 billion stars in the universe. For every star, there is the possibility of a surrounding family of planets. Yet not a single planet's existence has been confirmed outside our solar system. One of the long-term goals of spaceflight will be to find planets of other stars on which humans could settle and live freely and comfortably. With the rapidly increasing number of human beings, earth cannot support the entire human race forever—population pressures will steadily increase. If human civilizations were established on other planets, those people who have pioneering spirits would have the opportunity to migrate to new frontiers. There is also the possibility, because of human hatred, greed for power, and aptitude for making mistakes, that a nuclear war could completely destroy our form of life on earth; however, if the human race were living on a number of different planets scattered around the galaxy, our survival would be assured.

Toward the close of summer in 1986, NASA expects to launch a telescope into space that will open the doors to the universe. The Hubble Space Telescope, named after Edwin P. Hubble, the American astronomer who realized in 1925 that the universe is organized into differ-

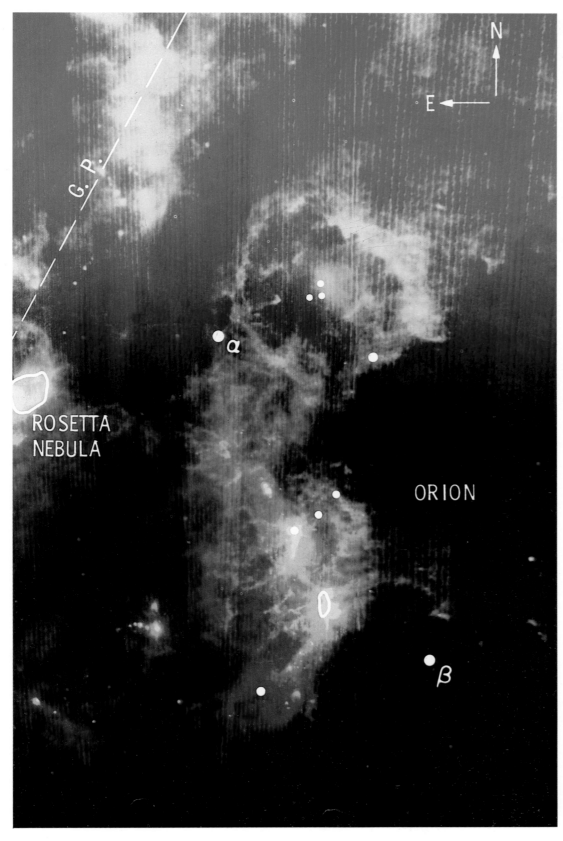

This false-color image of the region of sky around the constellation Orion was produced from data from the Infrared Astronomical Satellite and shows a much different view than that seen from optical telescopes. The intensity of radiation is represented by colors, with red being the strongest and blue the weakest. The Orion molecular cloud is visible (large feature dominating lower half of picture), located in and surrounding the sword of Orion. Part of the Milky Way crosses the upper left corner. Extended infrared cirrus clouds associated with the galaxy are also seen throughout the image.

ent galaxies, will be delivered by the Space Shuttle to an orbit 300 miles (480 km.) high. The telescope will become its own satellite, orbiting the earth six times. Its estimated visibility is 14 billion light-years, seven times farther than earth-based telescopes, and hardly comparable to the two million miles (3.2 million km.) we can see with the naked eye. Astronomers expect to see almost to the edge of the universe and the beginning of time; they anticipate revelations that could change our concepts of cosmic history, the universe's destiny, and of ourselves. This space instrument may bring us, for the first time, confirmation that there are planets that orbit around other stars, and thus raise the odds that we are not alone.

Because of the possibility that these planets do exist, it stands to reason that somewhere in the universe there must be conditions similar to earth's that would produce intelligent life. After all, the same atoms and molecules that are found within our solar system are also found at enormous distances from earth. If, indeed, we do make contact with a civilization that is more advanced than we are, who's to say they would be interested in us? In a "B.C." comic strip, Thor says to his companion:

> "I believe people of superior intelligence exist on other planets."
> "If that is so, why haven't they tried to contact us?" his friend asks.
> "Because of their superior intelligence."

Regardless of their intelligence, can anyone predict what they will look like? According to Carl Sagan, the individual

Stars of the North Pole.

circumstances of the earth's evolution that influence the way we look could not possibly be repeated anywhere else. Bearing in mind that it is highly unlikely that another civilization is going to resemble us—even in minute ways—are human beings capable of overlooking another life form's physical appearance in order to better understand it? Given our proclivity to judge harshly those who act or appear different from us, the evidence is stacked against us. Unless we can accept the differences among ourselves, we are going to have a hard time making friends with anything new, especially if they make the same mistakes we do.

We have already begun the effort to communicate with extraterrestrial civilizations. In March 1972, the *Pioneer 10* was launched to explore the environment of the planet Jupiter, and then to proceed out of the solar system toward a point on the celestial sphere near the boundary of the constellations Taurus and Orion. It is hoped that the spacecraft will be encountered by an extraterrestrial civilization that has mastered interstellar space flight and is able to intercept and capture space runaways.

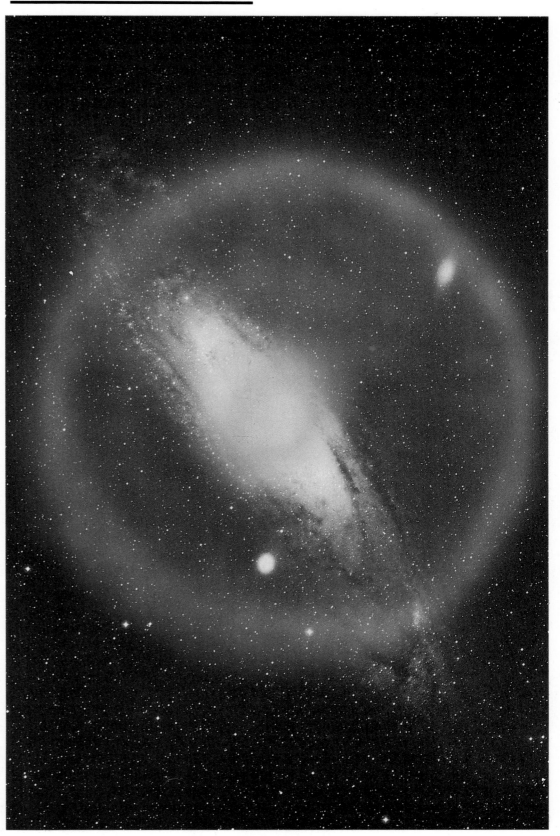

Artist's concept of a spherical halo— consisting of subatomic particles known as neutrinos—around our galaxy, emitting ultraviolet light. Neutrinos surround our galaxy in countless billions and were produced in the first few moments of creation. Originally it was thought that they contained no mass, like photons, but ultraviolet astronomical observations have shown evidence of decaying neutrinos, which indicates that they do have mass.

Spiral Galaxy NGC 6946. In a spiral galaxy, the gas, dust, and stars in the disk of the galaxy (together with any associated planets and their satellites) are all in orbit around a common center, (facing page). Like the planets in the solar system, the gas and stars move in response to the combined gravitational attraction of all the other mass.

Echo Satellite trail in the Milky Way. Some two hundred billion suns make up the Milky Way Galaxy, (right). We are located so far from the center of the Milky Way that it takes light, traveling at 186,000 miles per second—about 30,000 years—to reach us from there.

Crab Nebula. A diffuse, gaseous nebula in the constellation Taurus, Crab Nebula is the remnant of a supernova observed in 1054 by the Chinese and Japanese, (below). The nebula is a strong emitter of radio waves and at its center is an optical pulsar.

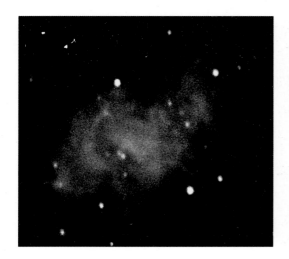

Center of Andromeda Galaxy M31. The large spiral galaxy nearest our own has been a laboratory for the study of the evolution of stars. Andromeda is believed to contain some 400 billion stars.

Attached to the antenna support struts is a message from earth that communicates the locale and the epoch whence the spacecraft came, and the nature of the spacecraft builders. It is written in scientific numerical code except for the description of the builders, which is a drawing of a man and a woman. Like Adam and Eve, the couple are unclothed. The man's hand is raised in a salutory greeting.

Another attempt at extraterrestrial communication is the radio telescope of the National Astronomy and Ionosphere Center in Arecibo, Puerto Rico. One

thousand feet (304.8 m.) in diameter, the telescope can communicate over tens of thousands of light-years with an identical copy of itself anywhere in the Milky Way galaxy. (It is assumed that a civilization interested in contacting others would also know about radio astronomy and about the structure of our galaxy.) So far the telescope has met only silence but the Milky Way is so vast that it could take light years before a signal is received, much less returned.

The Milky Way contains over 200 billion stars, most of which are concentrated in a disk. Around and between the

Galaxy NGC 7217, Type Sb, in Pegasus, (left). Although the forms of spiral galaxies are very diverse, astronomers have been able to classify them into three main groups. Galaxies designated as "Sa" have a large central bulge surrounded by tightly woven smooth arms in which bright "knots" are barely visible. "Sb" galaxies have a less noticeable central bulge and more open arms with more pronounced knots. "Sc" galaxies have a small central bulge and well-separated arms dotted with distinct luminous segments.

Ring Nebula in Lyra, (below). The most famous of the planetary nebulas, this one consists of a shell of gas separated from and expanding from a central star. Lyra is a northern constellation, that reaches its highest point in the evening sky in August.

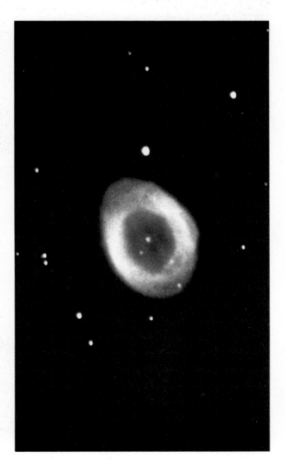

Galaxy NGC 7331, (above). Disk galaxies can be divided into two broad categories: spiral systems and SO systems. Both kinds of galaxies have a central bulge and a surrounding disk. The disks of spiral galaxies have visually prominent arms because they are studded with bright, newly formed stars. The disks of SO galaxies are smooth, show no spiral structure and are devoid of young stars. NGC 7331 represents a spiral disk.

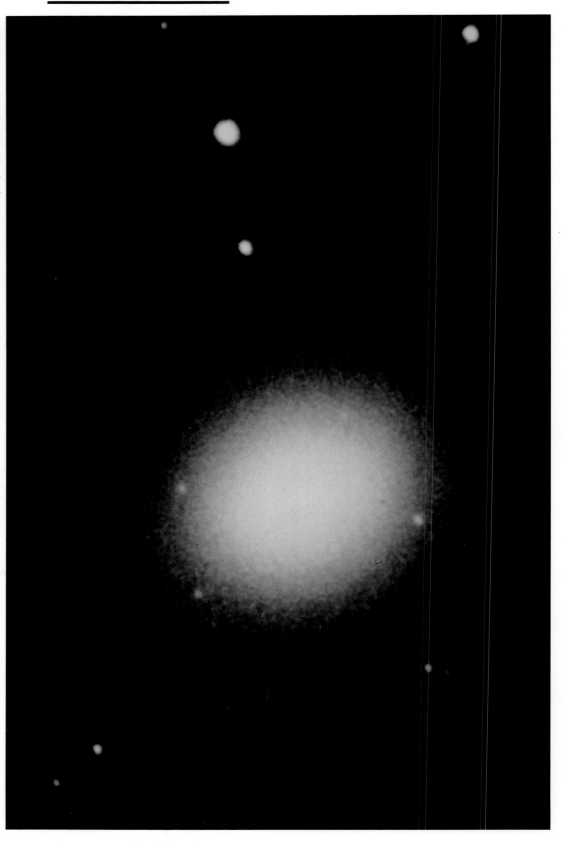

Galaxy M32, (right). One of the four companions of the Andromeda Galaxy.

stars are enormous quantities of dust that prevent us from seeing the galaxy's center. The earth sits in the central plane of the galaxy's band. Our solar system, however, is far from the center of the galaxy; the distance from the sun to the center is 8,500 parsecs. (One parsec is equal to 3.26 light-years.) Along with the rest of the mass in the central plane, the solar system revolves around the center of the galaxy. The sun makes a complete revolution every 200 million years. If we could look down at the Milky Way from above the galactic North Pole, we would see that the galaxy has a spiral structure like a nautilus seashell. The structure is not static—the many arms of the galaxy rotate above the galactic center. Our sun is located on the arm of Orion.

Spiral galaxies are mostly invisible, consisting of a huge outer halo that emits no light surrounding a smaller, visible disk. The halo contains most of the mass of the galaxy, a fact which puzzles scientists who haven't come up with a plausible idea of what material makes up this mass and, thus, most of the matter in the universe.

Edge-On Galaxy NGC 5907, (above). An example of a spiral disk galaxy.

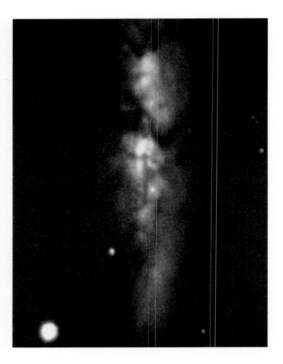

Galaxy M82 with active nucleus, (above). Active galaxies, which make up a very small number of all known galaxies, radiate as much as a million times more energy than typical galaxies. The emissions from an active galaxy extend over many frequencies, including gamma rays, x rays, visible radiation, infrared radiation, and radio waves. The question of what powers the active galaxy is being studied.

Nebula M16, (facing page). Nebulas are immense bodies of rarified gas and dust in interstellar spaces of galaxies. Diffuse nebula and planetary nebula are major classifications of these. Diffuse nebulas appear as light or dark clouds, have an irregular shape, and range up to 100 light-years in diameter. Planetary nebulas appear through telescopes as small disks with well-defined boundaries. Both consist of a shell of gaseous material surrounding a central hot star that emits radiation, which causes this material to glow.

Galaxy NGC 205, (left). One of the companion galaxies of the Andromeda Galaxy. It lies above the central bulge of Andromeda's center.

Orion Nebula M42, (facing page). Located near the middle of the sword hanging from Orion's belt, Orion Nebula is an enormous cloud of gas surrounding several stars. Its central bright region is about one degree in diameter, and it has a total extension of three degrees. It is about 1,600 light-years distant and 60 light-years in diameter.

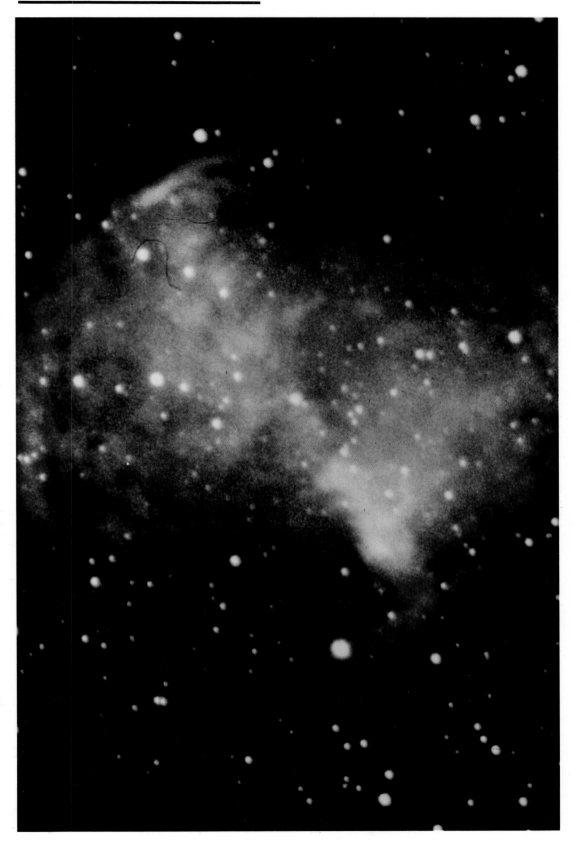

Galaxies are not arranged randomly but tend to exist in groups and clusters. Our galaxy belongs to the Local Group, which extends out for about one mega-parsec and has about two dozen identified members. The Magellanic Clouds are our closest neighbors at just over 50 kiloparsecs away. The Andromeda galaxy is the largest member of the Local Group, followed by the Milky Way and the M33. The others are considerably smaller.

Andromeda, containing 400 billion stars, is twice as large as the Milky Way. At a distance of two million light years from our solar system, it is the closest spiral galaxy to our own and, because it is much easier to see than our own galaxy, has been used to study the evolution of stars and galaxies.

Dumbell Nebula M27, (right).

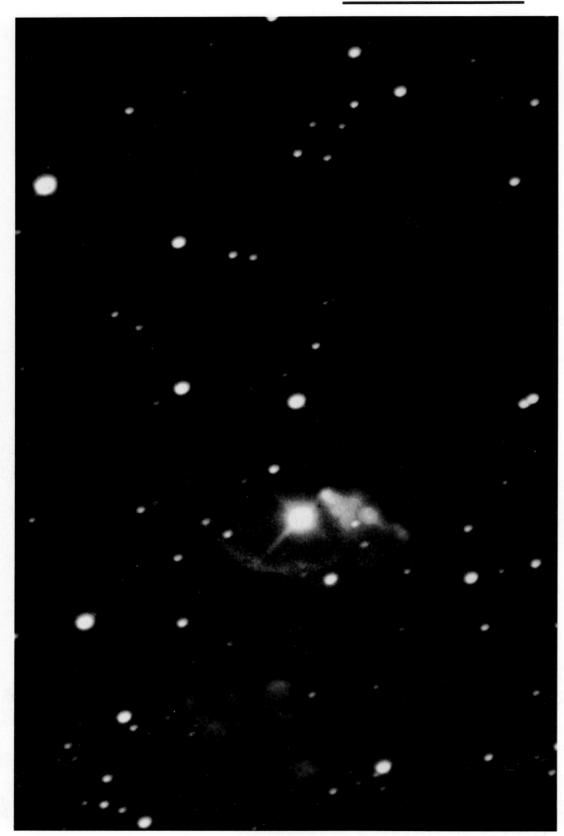

Nebula NGC 7635, (left).

Stars are born from giant clouds of gas and dust. They have evolved over billions of years, slowly turning hydrogen into helium in their deep interiors, converting the slight mass difference into energy, and sprinkling the sky with light. Every star in the sky is a sun—a potential center for life in space. The birth of stars theoretically generates a family of planets. The lives of the stars provide the energy upon which planetary life depends. Even the death of stars sets the stage for the continuation of life elsewhere in the galaxy.

The lifetime of a star depends on its mass; heavy stars burn the brightest, using up their nuclear fuel quickest. Our planet earth, a tiny hunk of rock and metal, circles a star whose life is half over. If our sun were only a quarter heavier, it would have been extinguished already. According to Carl Sagan, when the time does come for our sun to die, all life forms still in existence at that time will die with it, and our entire solar system will be transformed into a system more biologically advanced than our own.

Trifid Nebula M20, (facing page).

chapter five
PEOPLE IN SPACE

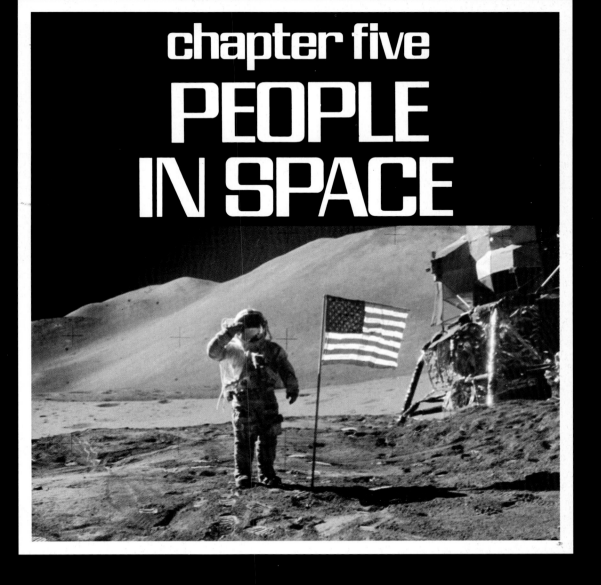

The most beautiful thing we can experience is the mysterious.
It is the source of all true art and science.

—Albert Einstein

(Previous page) Astronaut David R. Scott salutes the United States flag posted on the moon. Part of the Lunar Module is on the right. The Hadley Delta mountain is in the background.

PEOPLE IN SPACE

Sometime in the very near future, anyone who is healthy enough to fly in an airplane will be able to board the Space Shuttle and ride into orbit. Society Expeditions is already taking reservations. For a mere $1,000,000 per person, you can spend three days aboard a Space Shuttle flight, orbiting the earth sixteen times a day, participating in scientific experiments, living and working as part of an astronaut team, and bringing home photos of your trip that no one can top.

"Project Space Voyage" is scheduled for the mid-1990s. Granted, the price alone is going to limit the first group of passengers to wealthy executives, heiresses, and rock stars, but by and by we'll all get our turn. Eventually the Space Shuttle will resemble a tour bus with families, spry old ladies, high-school students and Japanese businessmen on board chatting excitedly. Flight atten-

Astronaut Ed White performing extravehicular activity.

Apollo 8 Commander Frank Borman four hours before he is launched on a lunar orbital mission. A technician is inserting pens to be used inflight in his spacesuit pocket.

A family photograph of astronaut Charles M. Duke, Jr., his wife, and two kids lies on the lunar surface. Duke, the Apollo 16 lunar module pilot, left the photo there during extravehicular activity on the final Apollo mission.

Astronaut Walter M. Schirra relaxes aboard the NASA Motor Vessel Retriever. Schirra is the first pilot to have flown during three generations of spacecraft— Mercury, Gemini, and Apollo.

dants will serve macaroni and cheese, rehydrated with a water gun. The pilot will introduce himself over the intercom in that easy Yaegerian drawl, "Ladies and gentlemen, this is your captain speaking, we are flying at an altitude of 200 miles, some 320 kilometers, above the earth, on your right is the continent of Asia..." and everyone will sit back and enjoy themselves, their belongings stored in lockers, their suit jackets or sweaters Velcroed to the walls.

After the "Fasten Your Seatbelt" sign is turned off, people will congregate in the Space Shuttle lounge to sip drinks, play video games, and socialize. Perhaps it may even be vaguely reminiscent of an airport or a Holiday Inn cocktail lounge with fiery orange carpeting, a fake teakwood bar, and as an added touch, red walls covered with photographs of the first astronauts. Will anyone on board remember what it was like for those men?

They were America's superheroes—in the same league as Orville and Wilbur Wright and Christopher Columbus. Before their missions, no one knew what space was like, what these men were going to find, or if they were ever going to be heard from again. Prior to sending men up into space, NASA had sent chimpanzees that had gone through months of

Apollo 7 astronauts, left to right, Walter M. Schirra, Donn F. Eisele, and Walter Cunningham, joke aboard the USS Essex following their splashdown.

Walter Cunningham, one of the original seven "right stuff" astronauts, takes time out for some playful joking around during Desert Survival Training.

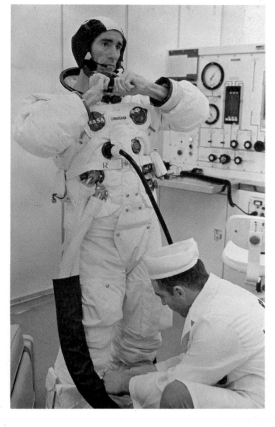

Astronaut Walter Cunningham is carefully suited up for his Apollo 7 mission.

The expressions on Apollo 7 astronauts Eisele, Schirra, and Cunningham's faces reflect a nation's pride as they are congratulated by President Lyndon B. Johnson via ship-to-shore telephone shortly after the capsule's splashdown.

Astronaut Walter Schirra in his pressure suit for the fifth manned spaceflight.

Astronaut M. Scott Carpenter ready for liftoff in the Mercury Aurora 7.

Virgil "Gus" Grissom, one of the original seven astronauts, was killed in a flashfire during preflight testing.

Astronauts John H. Glenn, Jr. and Neil Armstrong take a precious few minutes to relax in their jungle abode during Tropic Survival Training.

intensive training. Even up in space, however, they had tiny electrodes fastened to the soles of their feet—if they made a wrong move they would get corrected with an electric charge. Although there was the taunting and chiding from Edwards Air Force Base that the astronauts were "gonna follow monkeys into space," the use of chimps was not a comment on the intelligence of the astronauts—it was more the typical human response of "Let's try it out on something more expendable first."

NASA didn't care whether the astronauts were scientific geniuses or had Ph.D.'s in astrophysics and exobiology. They wanted tough-minded men in top physical condition. And so the original seven astronauts—Alan B. Shepard, Jr., John Glenn, Scott Carpenter, Walter Schirra, Gus Grissom, Donald Slayton, and L. Gordon Cooper—came from the ranks of the Air Force. They were fighter pilots who had logged over two thousand hours of flight time in state-of-the-art jets—clean-cut superjocks right off the fields of America's football stadiums.

They were put through every possible psychological and physical test that the men in white lab coats could put them through: claustrophobia tests, treadmill tests, the centrifuge machine with its G-forces; they even sent the candidates to the jungles of Central America to tough it out. But there were moments of glory, too: ticker-tape parades through the streets of New York City where Irish cops, Hari Krishna, Wall Street types, Chinese factory workers, the rich and fa-

John Glenn gives the ready sign for Mercury Friendship 7 *launch.*

Astronaut James A. Lovell, Jr., pilot of the Gemini 7, *is hoisted from the water by a recovery helicopter.*

mous thronged the streets waving and cheering and crying. People hung out every window shredding any paper they could find (including phone books) and tossed them into the air like confetti.

All the candidates were equally qualified, and so when the moment came to choose the first astronaut to go into space, it became a personality contest. John Glenn looked like he had an excellent chance because he was America's favorite. Sandy-haired, freckle-faced, he could have been in a Kellogg's Corn Flakes commercial as a boy. Glenn also had the wit and charm to always say the right thing to reporters, and he appealed to the core of America—he was a good Christian and a devout family man.

But Alan B. Shepard, Jr., the natural-born leader and the only one with an impressive military title, got the position. Shepard, though hard-pressed to show it, was thrilled! On the morning of May 5, 1961, he blasted off in *Freedom 7* to become America's first astronaut. Later he admitted that it was an emotional experience which changed his life dramatically. "I was a rotten S.O.B. before I left, now I'm just an S.O.B."

John Glenn was chosen for the next flight in February of 1962. His *Mercury 6* capsule, the *Friendship 7,* pierced through the earth's atmosphere and made Glenn the first American astronaut to orbit our planet. Shortly thereafter, astronaut Scott Carpenter was launched on an almost identical spaceflight. Whereas Glenn stuck to basic mission plans, Carpenter was instructed by NASA's life scientists to perform some experiments while orbiting the earth. Of the original seven, Carpenter was the most science-minded; he was also the most romantic and philosophical. Being in space was an adventure for him. He spinned and twirled through space, spotted an array of shimmering dust particles over Mexico, and barely had time to complete his list of experiments before returning to earth. Fuel was running dangerously low and NASA ordered him to return to earth immediately. But in the next second he

The boyish, all-American face of John Glenn, right after his successful three-orbit flight.

Alan B. Shepard, Jr., prepares for the first manned suborbital flight.

Apollo 11 astronauts Neil Armstrong and Michael Collins through the window of their Mobile Quarantine Facility following splashdown and recovery.

Astronaut Scott Carpenter embraces his friend and fellow astronaut John Glenn after Carpenter's near-disastrous mission in which his craft veered off course. Mission Control's communications black out with Carpenter nearly led NASA, Walter Cronkite, and the nation to believe they had met their first in-space tragedy.

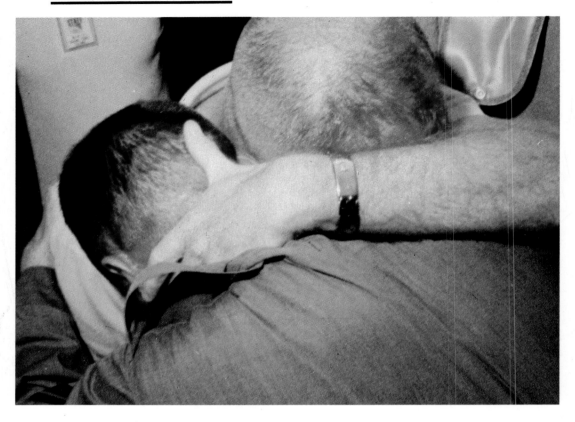

Astronaut Neil Armstrong, Apollo 11 commander, inside the Lunar Module during its stay on the lunar surface.

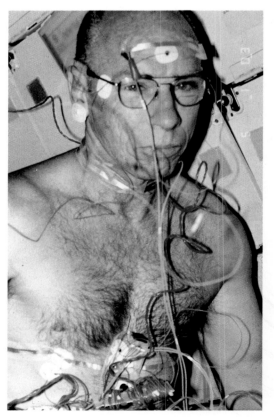

Dr. Thornton undergoes self-conducted medical testing onboard the Space Shuttle Challenger.

was gone; there was no sound from the *Aurora 7;* Scott Carpenter was lost in space. Flight control couldn't believe it—NASA had lost a man! An official was summoned to call Carpenter's wife. Walter Cronkite, reporting the flight on CBS News, was starting to choke up and tears welled in his eyes. It was no secret now.

Then, just as mysteriously as he had disappeared, Scott Carpenter burst through the earth's atmosphere and plunged into the Atlantic Ocean 125 miles (200 km.) northeast of Puerto Rico—miles away from the cape. NASA was furious! But Glenn, Carpenter's closest astronaut-buddy, greeted Scott with an embrace that betokened everyone's true feelings. After that flight there was no more ad-libbing, no life science experiments, just do your job and come back...period. Carpenter's flight stood as a bad example for the astronauts who were waiting for their turns to go up in space.

The most tragic accident for NASA occurred during the preflight testing of the first manned Apollo mission, *Apollo 13.* Astronauts Gus Grissom, Edward White, and Roger Chaffee were suited up in the command module, moving through the countdown toward a simulated launch. At T-minus-10 minutes tragedy struck. Observers heard one of the crewmen report that there was a fire aboard the spacecraft. Ground crew members saw a flash fire break through the spacecraft shell and envelope the spacecraft in smoke. The rescue attempt took five minutes—by the time they were able to get the hatch open from the outside, the astronauts were dead from asphyxiation.

Despite this tragic incident, the astronauts-in-training remained undaunted, and competition amongst them to be the first men on the moon was fierce. Astronauts Neil Armstrong, Edwin "Buzz" Aldrin, and Michael Collins were selected. Armstrong was chosen to command with Aldrin as co-pilot; Collins was to stay in the Apollo rocket and circle the moon. The original plans were for co-pilot Al-

Astronaut Ronald McNair, Mission Specialist, in the middeck of the Challenger.

Astronaut Gerald Carr, Skylab 4 *Mission Commander, tests the automatically stabilized maneuvering unit (ASMU) in the forward compartment of the Skylab space station.*

107

drin to take the first step onto the lunar surface, but Armstrong exercised his authority as ship commander and rewrote the script, putting himself first and thus causing considerable friction between the two men.

The astronauts of today are cast from a different mold. No longer must they all fit the boy-next-door/superhero image. In general, they're a little older, have degrees in fields such as astro-geophysics and backgrounds in solar-terrestrial observations.

In the mid-1970s NASA put out an announcement soliciting applications for new astronauts. They advertised that they wanted women and minorities to apply. About eight thousand people answered the ad, out of which two hundred finalists were selected. Thirty-five were then chosen based on their application, health record, and references. Of those thirty-five, all were white, six were women, and one of these women was Dr. Sally K. Ride.

Ride was finishing her Ph.D. in physics when she applied. She is not sure why she was selected; she says NASA never tells anyone why they were chosen or what they are looking for. Ride considers herself a normal, healthy person who loves sports. She was not searching for fame and considers the publicity part of the job to be the most difficult. When asked how her experience compared to that found in the movie, *The Right Stuff,* Dr. Ride replied that the program is dif-

Astronaut Edwin Aldrin, Jr., standing on the lunar surface during Apollo 11 *extravehicular experiments.*

The STS-9/Spacelab 1 crew from left to right: Pilot Brewster Shaw, Commander John Young, Mission Specialists Owen Garriott and Robert Parker, and Payload Specialists Ulf Merbold and Byron Lichtenberg.

Scientist-astronaut Owen K. Garriott reconstitutes a prepackaged container of food in the crew quarters of Skylab 3 space station.

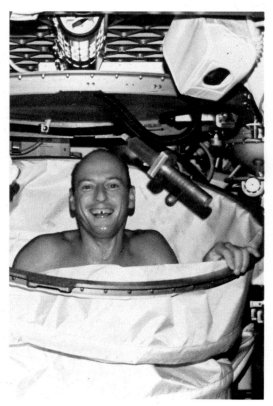

Commander Charles Conrad, Jr., after a hot shower in the crew quarters of Skylab 2.

Mission Specialist Judith Resnik positions herself on the floor of the Discovery's middeck to note items on a clipboard pad.

Astronaut Aldrin poses for this photograph beside the deployed American flag during Apollo 11 extravehicular activity. To the left is the lunar module. The footprints visible on the surface of the moon will remain fixed there, unlike footprints in the earth's soil, which will erode due to wind and water.

ferent today. The centrifuge machine with its G-forces is gone, and along with it much of the rigorous, physical testing.

Today's "right stuff" for astronauts is mental muscle. They need to learn all about the Space Shuttle and the experiments they'll be performing. It's an eight-to-sixteen-hour-a-day job that lasts for ten months. There's no required physical conditioning, but there is enough peer pressure involved so that before a flight, everybody starts exercising to get into shape.

There are about ninety astronauts today; half that number has gone into space and want to go again. The other half eagerly awaits its turn. No one, however, could have been more thrilled to be given the chance to orbit the earth than "teachernaut" Christa McAuliffe, who was chosen from ten thousand applicants. Honored with parades and trophies just like the original seven in the early days, she has become a national hero simply by being the first "everyday citizen" to go into space. Perhaps by plotting the way for the rest of us, she represents—even more than those before her—the day when we'll all have the chance to witness firsthand the mysteries of space.

Astronaut Bruce McCandless II tests the foot restraint mechanism on the end of the remote manipulator system. In his hand is a tool bag.

The crew of the STS 61-A, Spacelab D-1, Messerschmid, Merbold and Furrer clown in the foreground while Dunbar and Bluford look on.

chapter six
SPACE EQUIPMENT

From a wild weird clime that lieth, sublime,
Out of Space—Out of Time.

—Edgar Allan Poe

SPACE EQUIPMENT

On the tenth voyage of the Space Shuttle, Mission Specialist Bruce McCandless II donned a Manned Maneuvering Unit (MMU) and became the first human to fly in formation with the Orbiter *Challenger* through a full circumnavigation of the earth at a speed of 17,500 miles (28,000 km.) per hour. In the days to follow, McCandless and fellow Mission Specialist Robert Stewart both acted as human satellites, moving as far as 300 feet (480 km.) away from the Orbiter without the protection of tethers or life-support umbilical lines. McCandless and Stewart had the courageous task of checking out the MMU's performance; they also demonstrated their ability to use the system effectively. MMUs are going to play a big role in future space operations. They will be employed in missions involving retrieval, repair, and service of satellites in orbit, and eventually they'll be used in combination with free-flying robot vehicles to assemble the future manned space station.

The MMU is an orbital propulsion sys-

(Previous page) Astronaut Bruce McCandless II, at maximum distance from the earth-orbiting Space Shuttle Challenger, *is in the midst of the first field tryout of the nitrogen-propelled, hand-controlled backpack called the manned maneuvering unit (MMU).*

On its third day in orbit, the Discovery *began its operations with this giant solar array experiment panel.*

SPACE EQUIPMENT

Astronaut Bruce McCandless II is a few meters away from the cabin of the earth-orbiting Space Shuttle Challenger. *This spacewalk was the first use of and demonstrated the advantages of the MMU, which allows for greater mobility than tethers.*

The Tiros Operational Satellite spacecraft is shown in final checkout prior to being launched. The satellite provides daily coverage of weather systems around the globe.

SATCOMIII, the 1,950 lb. spacecraft, undergoes prelaunch checkout at Cape Canaveral. SATCOM was the first 24-channel communications satellite devoted to relaying signal-to-cable TV installations in the United States.

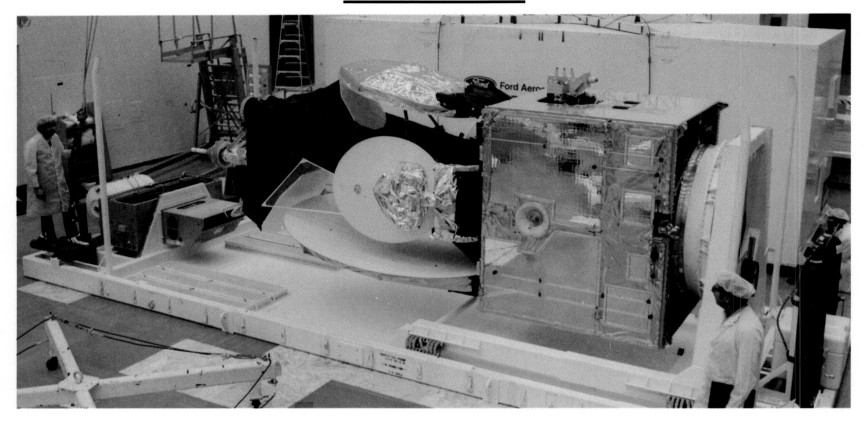

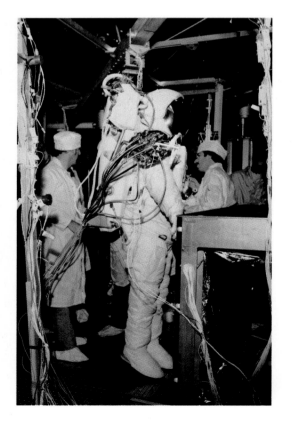

INTELSAT V, the largest and most powerful communications satellite built to date, can relay up to 12,000 two-way telephone calls and color TV channels simultaneously. The technicians here begin the meticulous job of uncrating and assembling the satellite.

Suit technicians prepare a pressurized extravehicle mobility unit (EMU). These suits, along with the MMU, have revolutionized the work astronauts are able to do outside the spacecraft.

The Challenger's *flight test article is suspended on the end of a remote manipulator system over the payload bay. Fleecy white clouds and the Atlantic Ocean provide a dramatic backdrop.*

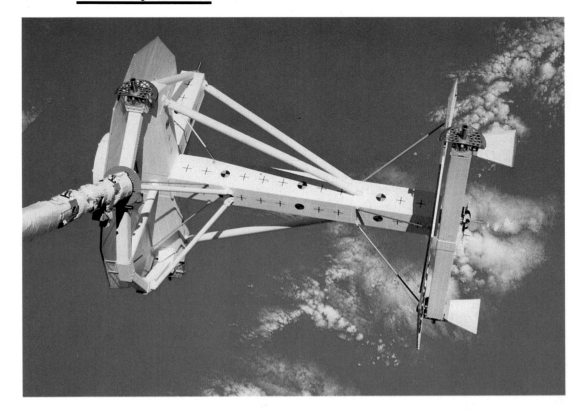

tem in which twenty-four small nitrogen gas jets provide thrusting impulses that maneuver an astronaut in any desired direction. Gas is fed into the thrusters from two tanks that hold thirteen pounds (4.85 kg.) of nitrogen. The tanks can be recharged in the Orbiter's bay in less than twenty minutes. Hand controllers built into the unit's armrests provide the means by which one operates. The left hand control governs fore/aft, right/left, and up/down movements; the right hand controls roll, pitch, and yaw motions. The controls can be used singly or in combination to provide a full range of motion—or a total of 729 command combinations. Two MMU batteries provide enough electrical power for six hours of extravehicular activity.

By itself, the MMU is not considered a one-person spacecraft because it has no life-support equipment. In order to employ the MMU, an astronaut must wear the Extravehicular Mobility Unit (EMU) spacesuit/backpack and latch the MMU onto the backpack. The EMU supplies oxygen, removes carbon dioxide, controls temperature, and provides protection from meteoroids.

The astronauts of the tenth Space Shuttle flight also used another new device called the Manipulator Foot Restraint (MFR). The MFR is a work platform that attaches to the end of the Remote Manipulator System (RMS), the 50-foot-long (15.24 m.) robot arm. Foot restraints and a safety tether keep the astronaut in place on the platform, leaving his arms free to work.

The solar array experiment panel for the Discovery's *payload stands against the darkness of space as it heads toward a sunrise scene. The vertical stabilizer of* Discovery *is silhouetted against the panel.*

The Skylab space station cluster in earth orbit, taken from Skylab 3 command service module. Note that one of the two solar array system wings is missing.

Spacelab 2 undergoing functional checkout of its 10 pallet-mounted experiments in the Level 4 workstand of the Operations and Checkout Building. Shown in this picture are the twin x-ray telescopes, the conical lens of the infra-red telescope, the large egg-shaped cosmic ray detector, and the Igloo—a pressurized container for the avionics needed to operate and control Spacelab systems.

NASA is preparing the Solar Maximum Mission for earth orbit. The satellite, carrying seven scientific instruments, is designed to provide scientists with pictures of solar flares—violent eruptions on the sun's surface—in the ultraviolet and gamma ray regions of the spectrum.

Another new piece of space equipment is the Trunnion Pin Attachment Device, or TPAD. This device is a docking mechanism that is affixed to the MMU armrests and enables the astronaut to dock at free-flying satellites and, in effect, become a part of the satellite. Using the MMU thrusters, the astronaut can stabilize the satellite for the Orbiter's RMS to lock onto the satellite and deposit it in the payload bay.

As many interesting innovations are occurring inside the Space Shuttle as on the outside. Consider Spacelab: a 23-foot-long (7 m.) module that acts as a convertible laboratory designed to accommodate scientists and their instruments in low-earth orbit. In Spacelab, scientists are using new tools and techniques to gaze at the sun and stars, probe the gases that surround the earth, and examine materials and living organisms outside of the earth's gravity. They are being treated to a dramatically improved view of all the remote, minute, and otherwise invisible details of nature. They also have the advantage of bringing very large instruments on board Spacelab and taking film, tapes, plants, experiment samples, and other data home for analysis.

Beginning with the *Spacelab 1* mission in 1983, the orbiting laboratory has been used for research in various fields of science. *Spacelab 2* continues with investigations in solar physics, atmospheric physics, high-energy astro-

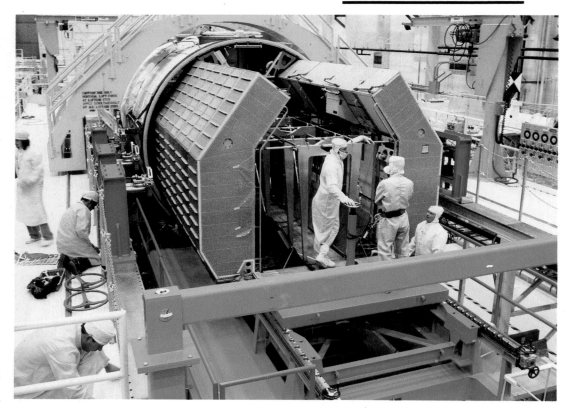

The experiment racks and flight floor are inserted inside the pressurized module that will make up a part of Spacelab 3. Nine of the thirteen experiments that will fly aboard the mission are contained in the experiment racks.

Mission Specialist Dr. Norman E. Thagard familiarizes himself with the EMU onboard NASA's zero-gravity aircraft. Dr. Thagard has anchored his EMU to a lifeline while he and engineers await the next weightless session.

The Solar Maximum Mission, the first spacecraft designed specifically for the study of solar flares, represents a major step toward a better understanding of the violent nature of the sun and its effects on the earth.

A Mission Specialist, using the MMU, approaches the Solar Maximum Mission satellite to stabilize the satellite and make repairs. He holds a device with which he will grab the satellite and hold it steady.

With the added mobility provided by their manned maneuvering units, Space Shuttle astronauts erect a large structure for a future space station. Aboard the Space Shuttle's cargo bay is an automated beam builder that produces triangular girders of ultra-lightweight metal plate.

An astronaut prepares to dock with the Solar Maximum Mission satellite using the MMU backpack apparatus. His mission is to stabilize the tumbling satellite and bring it to the Shuttle's cargo bay for repairs.

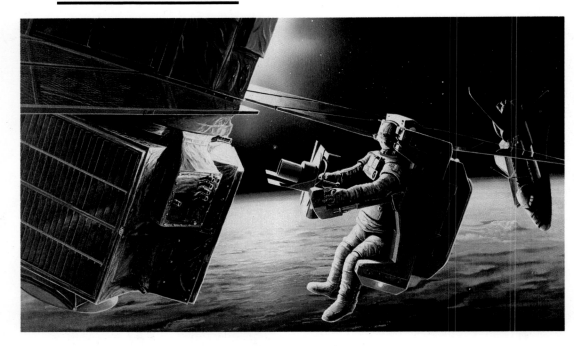

The Hubble Telescope, to be launched into orbit by the Space Shuttle, will enable scientists to gaze seven times farther than any other telescope into space—possibly to the edge of the universe.

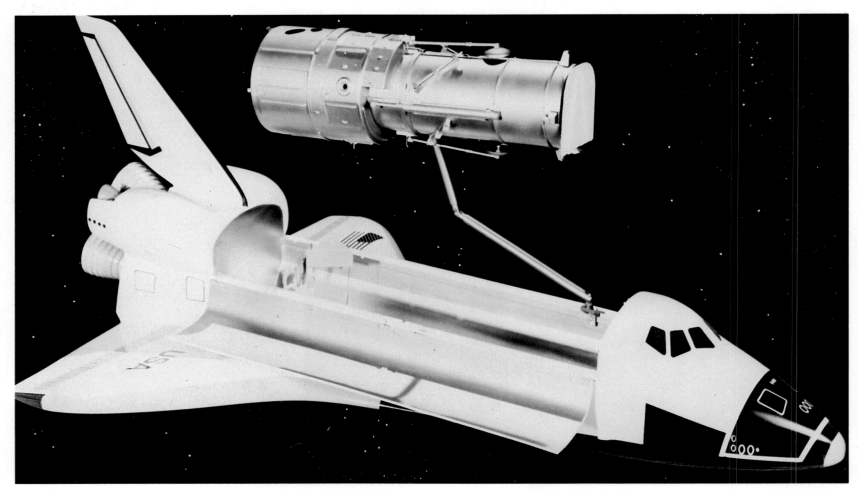

physics, infrared astronomy, plasma physics, and life sciences. Plasma physicists are interested in the high-energy processes that occur during magnetic storms and auroras that often disrupt our communication signals, navigation, and power transmissions. Instead of waiting for them to occur naturally, Spacelab scientists can artificially create auroras and thereby determine the exact environmental conditions before, during, and after such a disturbance. To imitate auroras, the investigators generate and accelerate electron beams into the atmosphere. Probes in the Shuttle monitor the resultant chemical and electrical processes as the beams are emitted.

Each Spacelab mission has a unique design appropriate to the mission's goals. A number of Spacelab configurations can be assembled from various standardized parts, such as habitable modules, an igloo, and exposed platforms called pallets. The igloo houses Spacelab subsystems for computer operations, data transmissions, and thermal control. This cylindrical, pressurized container is located directly outside the Shuttle cabin at the head of the pallet train. The pallets are used for experiments that require direct exposure to the space environment. Three pallets, an Instrument Pointing System (IPS), and a special support structure are the main Spacelab components.

On the first pallet, three solar instruments and one atmospheric instrument

Astronaut Bruce McCandless II demonstrates use of the extravehicular mobility unit. Here he is shown leaving the Space Shuttle.

Astronaut Bruce McCandless II used the combination of the remote manipulator system (RMS) arm and the mobile foot restraint to try out the "cherry picker" concept.

are mounted on the IPS. Whereas instruments used to be pointed toward particular celestial objects or areas by maneuvering the Shuttle to an appropriate altitude, the IPS can aim instruments more accurately by fixing on a target as the Shuttle continues to move in a fixed orbit. One plasma physics instrument, an electron beam generator, is also mounted on the first pallet. The second Spacelab pallet holds a large double x-ray telescope and three plasma physics detectors. The last pallet supports an infrared telescope, a superfluid helium technology experiment, and a small plasma diagnostics satellite. Aft of the pallet train, a huge, egg-shaped instrument called the cosmic ray detector is mounted in a specially designed support structure that is tilted to increase detector exposure to space.

Astronaut Irwin salutes the flag. The Lunar Module is in the center. The Lunar Rover is at the right.

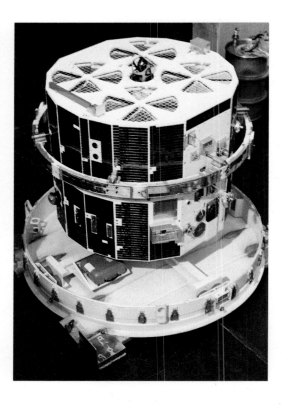

Atmosphere Explorer-D was the second in a series of three maneuverable, unmanned spacecraft to explore in detail an area of the earth's outer atmosphere where important energy transfer and chemical reactions take place.

An artist's concept of an artificially induced aurora, one of the seventy some experiments to fly aboard Spacelab 1. High-intensity electrons, ion beams, and neutral gas clouds are fired from accelerators into the space environment to illuminate the earth's invisible structure of magnetized plasma.

Ignition of the Space Shuttle's giant solid rocket boosters is achieved as they begin generating energy equivalent to 44 million horsepower.

Crew members control the pallet-mounted instruments via computer keyboards located in the aft flightdeck. From there, they also control the IPS and operate the Shuttle manipulator arm with a computer.

Spacelab represents a new phase in the evolution of science: the regular use of space as a suitable environment for laboratory research conducted by humans. As scientists equip laboratories aboard orbital platforms and space stations, major scientific and technological advances are expected.

The Space Telescope—the Edwin P. Hubble Space Telescope as it is formally called—is the most dramatic advance in astronomy since the invention of the telescope in 1610. This orbital observatory is scheduled to be shuttle-launched in 1986 and will be in operation at least until the year 2000—expanding the human view of the universe some 350 times. Even the most powerful telescopes on earth today can scope only a small part of the galaxy. The atmosphere, which acts as a veil, is the limiting factor that filters out most of the light and other radiations coming from space.

The telescope will operate unencumbered because it is 370 miles (592 km.) above the earth's atmosphere. It will allow us to see into space seven times farther than the most advanced earth-based telescopes, detecting objects fifty times fainter than anything ever seen before and returning images with ten times the clarity of previously used scopes.

The powerful crawler-transporter begins the six-hour journey from the Vehicle Assembly Building to the launch pad with the Space Shuttle, STS-4 external tank, and the solid rocket booster in tow.

Columbia's *remote manipulator system (RMS) arm and hand-like device grasp a multi-instrument monitor that detects contaminants in the environment. The North Atlantic Ocean southeast of the Bahamas serves as the backdrop.*

STS-4 thunders away from launch pad bound for a seven-day earth-orbital mission.

The Hubble Telescope will orbit the earth at an altitude of 310 miles and will observe stars and galaxies that are one-fiftieth as bright as the stars that are now observed by the largest ground-based telescopes.

The remote manipulator system (RMS) arm suspends the giant Long Duration Exposure Facility high above the Gulf of Mexico before releasing it into space. Carried into earth orbit by the Space Shuttle Challenger, LDEF will remain in space for ten months.

Light from distant galaxies takes an incredibly long time to reach us. Capturing light that began its cosmic course when the universe first began some 12 to 20 billion years ago, the space telescope will allow scientists to look back into time and will reveal enlightening clues to the origin and history of the universe.

The twelve-ton (10.884 metric tons), forty-three-foot (13.11 m.) Space Telescope works with mirrors. Starlight enters the open end of the observatory and is reflected from a large primary mirror to a smaller secondary mirror where it is magnified, sharply focused, and then directed to an instrument section. Here the images are photographed (sometimes taking hours of exposure) and analyzed. The images and instrument data are then relayed via a communications satellite to Goddard Space Flight Center, which will have the entire responsibility of controlling the telescope, processing the data, and sending it thirty miles away to the Space Telescope Science Institute. At the precise moment the images are beamed here astronomers from all over the world will be gathered to watch the images come over the consoles and perhaps, to witness the birth of time.

chapter seven
THE FUTURE IN SPACE

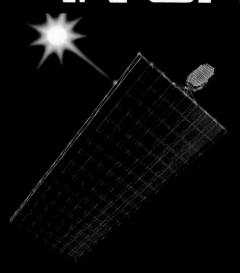
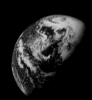

Predictions are very difficult to make,
especially when they deal with the future.

—Mark Twain

THE FUTURE IN SPACE

What *is* our future in space? What can we reasonably expect in the twenty-first century? Is the forecast an optimistic one or is it bleak? Everyone likes to speculate on the earth's future in space, and there are plenty of dismal predictions from all mediums. Take films, for example. In the last thirty years we've had *The Day the Earth Caught Fire*, *The Day the Earth Stood Still*, *The Day the Sky Exploded*, *The Day the World Ended*, *War Between the Planets*, and *Space Soldiers Conquer the Universe*, to name just a few.

Even comic books foretell the worst. In a recent issue of *Judge Dredd*, which sells to a surprising number of adult and teenage readers, future life on earth is described as follows: "No inhabitant of today can comprehend the sheer immensity of Mega-City #1 in the early twenty-second century. Over 800 million people—the population of a hundred Londons—crammed into vast city blocks, each housing over 60,000 citi-

(Previous page) An artist's rendition of a solar cell array with a transmitting antenna that will, it is hoped, direct energy to earth.

Twenty-first century space colony, depicted by artist Don Davis, is a nineteen-mile long cylinder containing trees, water, and air. Large, movable rectangular mirrors on the side of the cylinder direct sunlight into the interior, regulate the seasons, and control day-night cycles.

A resident of a twenty-first century space colony might see this vista of an earth-like landscape from inside his home in space. All materials used to construct such a colony would come from the moon or Asteroid Belt.

A space colony of this size could support a population of two hundred thousand to several million, depending on the design. In this large colony, earth-like gravity would be produced by the centrifugal force created by the rotation of the large cylinder around its long axis once every 114 seconds.

An artist's concept of the agricultural area of a space colony. On the top levels of the farm wheat, soybean, and sorghum would be grown. The bottom level is a drying facility. Water would be supplied directly from the river and indirectly through the fish tanks that line the sides. Altogether these tanks would hold 260,000 fish.

zens. . . . Each city block was a city within a city, from birth in the city block hospital to death in the city block crematorium, it was possible for a citizen to spend his entire lifetime without leaving his own block!"

Do we have good reason to be this gloomy or is it merely a fear of the unknown? Granted, the earth's population isn't getting any smaller, and unless a nuclear war, a national disaster of great proportions, or an epidemic wipes out a high percentage of the earth's inhabitants, visions such as "Mega-City #1" could become a reality. But if we look for a moment at the possibilities NASA predicts, the future looks anything but bleak.

At a recent seminar on space settlements, NASA experts and university professors kept the room buzzing as they discussed concepts for space colonies. One idea, proposed by Dr. Gerard O'Neill of Princeton University, was of a cylinder-shaped colony orbiting between the earth and the moon. It would be nineteen miles (30.4 km.) long and four miles (6.4 km.) in diameter, and would support a population of two hundred thousand to several million, depending on the design. All the materials used to construct such a colony would come from the moon or the asteroid belt and be manufactured in space using solar power. The interior could be made to resemble the designer's wishes, from the Rocky Mountains to the Oklahoma plains

Shown in this conception of an agricultural area with a lake and river are farming sections that are divided by three more populated areas. The louvres being installed would absorb cosmic radiation while allowing sunlight inside.

Capable of supporting several hundred thousand people, this colony would be 19 miles long (32 km.) and 4 miles (6,400 meters) in diameter. The bridge similar to the San Francisco Bay Bridge, is shown to emphasize eventual size of such a colony.

Stationed a quarter of a million miles from earth and constructed almost entirely of ore mined from the moon, this colony would contain trees, grassy parks and streams—all the comforts of our global home. Beneath the upper living area is a level of offices, stores, service buildings, and facilities for light industry.

Cut-away view of a proposed space habitat, fully shielded against cosmic rays by a spherical shell of lunar-made material.

With these attractive living areas, families relocated from the earth could remain in the settlement for several years. Without them, a high-cost space commuting service would be necessary and the prospect of living and working in space would be, from an economic standpoint, impossible.

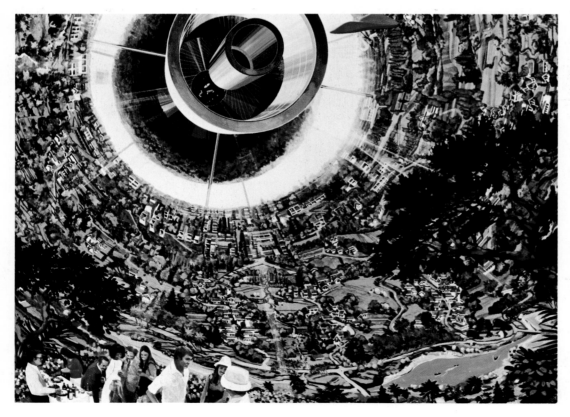

A small transportation vehicle awaits liftoff from a proposed mining settlement on the moon. Lunar materials will be the prime resource for metals and oxygen for space colonies. To the right of the vehicle are the mines and living quarters for the town. The lower tubes are agricultural sheds where food for the town will be grown. To the left, lunar materials speed down a magnetic track, which prevents them from being slowed down by lunar gravity.

THE FUTURE IN SPACE

An artist's concept of the interior of a space colony. The top deck is a view of a typical housing complex. The track shown is part of a larger transit system. The lower deck is a service area that will provide storage, power distribution, and processing equipment for light industry.

An exterior view of a space habitat for members of the workforce of a space manufacturing complex.

This drawing shows the inside of a living module envisioned for the Space Operation Center, a short-term facility for space workers.

This proposed NASA space colony for 10,000 inhabitants utilizes a wheel-like exterior of moon rocks to shield inhabitants from cosmic radiation. The mirror floating above the colony reflects sunlight into the colony's interior.

Material mined from the lunar surface would be processed into aluminum, glass, and other useful materials in this manufacturing facility. Located several miles from the colony itself, the two would be connected by a transport tube that would convey workers and supplies back and forth. The triangular wings are solar panels.

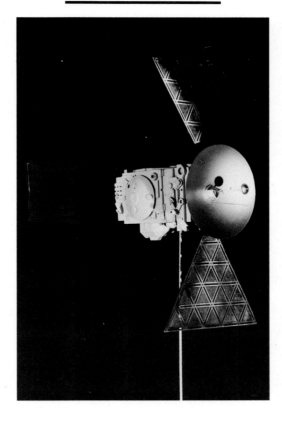

to the timber forests of Washington. The colony would have the same life-support system as the earth's: solar energy would supply power to the inhabitants while raw materials would be derived from lunar rocks or asteroids. Beaches would be made from lunar sand. Large movable rectangular mirrors on the side of the cylinder directed into the interior would regulate the seasons and control the day-night cycle. Earth-like gravity would be produced by centrifugal force from the cylinder rotating around its axis once every 114 seconds.

At the hub of the wheel, an inhabitant would be weightless. In this area, colonists could play low-gravity sports and use human-powered flying machines. Beneath the living and recreation area would be a level of stores, service buildings, offices, and industrial facilities. A separate area, exposed to the intense sunlight of space, would be set aside for the growing of crops, and could supply the total food requirements of the colony.

This scenario may sound farfetched, but scientists are convinced it's the direction in which we're heading. NASA is beckoning big business to try operations in the new high frontier of space by offering cut-rate shuttle prices, called "Getaway Specials," to commercial customers interested in space experimentation.

The temptation to manufacture in space is leading many experts to predict that it will be the site of the next industrial revolution. Many pharmaceuticals, crys-

An artist's drawing depicts a space colony approached from the moon, in which the central cylinder is 19 miles (32 km.) long. Ringing the endcap is a series of agricultural stations. Sunlight is directed into the central cylinder by the three movable rectangular strip mirrors, which control day-night cycles.

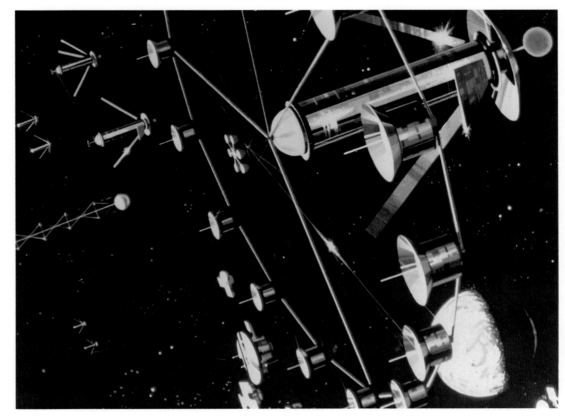

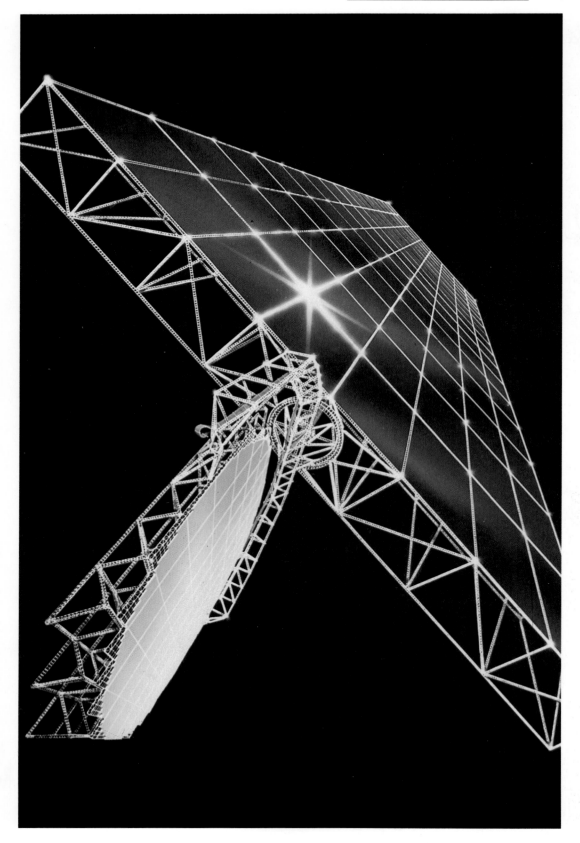

This is a NASA design for a permanent community in space. The outer "tire" is a radiation shield built of compressed lunar material made in much the same way a cinder block is formed. To simulate earth's gravity, the entire habitat rotates at one revolution per minute around the central hub.

The proposed solar power satellite shown here is being studied by NASA and the Department of Energy. The satellite would provide 5,000 megawatts of electrical power to a ground receiving station which would in turn feed into a commercial electrical power grid.

Shown is the McDonnell-Douglas space platform concept developed to its potential as a manned structure. This concept is being studied under contract to NASA.

This particular unmanned space station is composed of communications antennae, two solar arrays, a space radiator and several rotating pallets capable of holding space science and applications payloads.

Portrayed here is an artist's rendering of a space station concept. Next to an unmanned scientific pallet facing down toward earth are three modules, two manned for habitation and experimentation, and one unmanned facing upward that provides logistics support. A space station such as this would be launched and serviced by the Shuttle.

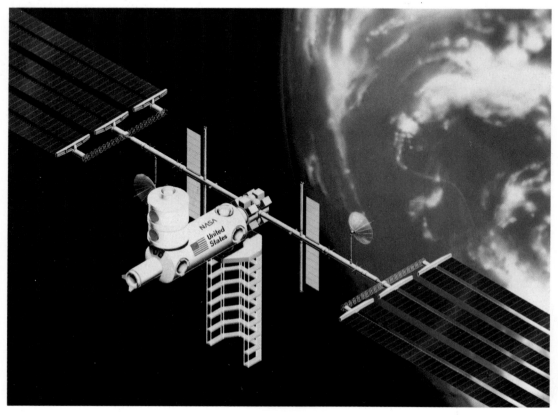

An enclosed space garage protects vehicles from floating debris or meteoroids.

tals, ceramics, and metal alloys that cannot be produced on earth can be manufactured in orbital factories. On earth, sedimentation and other effects of gravity impede the separation of certain biological materials into ultrapure forms as well as interfere with the formation of certain alloys and crystals. In space, however, it is possible to grow larger and more perfect crystals for use in semiconductors, solar cells, and other electronic devices; to produce incredibly pure glass for optical fibers and lasers; to develop lighter and stronger metals; and to produce more easily various hormones and enzymes for treating cancer, emphysema, and other diseases. With these incentives luring businesses to space, in-orbit manufacturing could become a $27 billion-a-year business by the turn of the century. And where large companies go, people usually follow.

With the Space Shuttle in full swing, the Space Station is the next logical step towards increasing the manufacturing and technological capabilities of the United States. Its development will assure the United States of continued leadership in space through the 1990s and beyond. The Space Station is multi-faceted: It will serve as a manufacturing plant for the production of materials not available on earth; as a scientific laboratory for research in earth sciences and solar system exploration; as a communi-

A free-flying power station that would support Space Shuttle flights of up to 120 days. An astronaut performing an extravehicular task puts the size of the power station in perspective.

This space station is a conceptualization of an unmanned space platform designed for servicing. Visible are the platform's rotating pallets capable of holding space science and applications payloads. Extending downward from the platform is a "hangar" device for the Space Shuttle; at lower right the Orbiter is shown docked with the platform.

This concept features living quarters with artificial gravity, control center, three zero-gravity modules, and an open-beam platform.

This rendering shows the Space Shuttle undergoing servicing at a space station. The Shuttle's remote manipulator system is deployed with a payload at an unmanned platform. Near the Orbiter are the platform's rotating pallets, which are capable of holding space science and applications payloads.

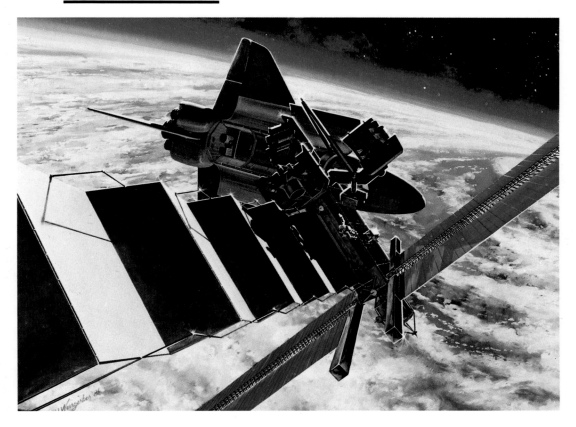

cations center; and as a facility for developing technology and materials--processing. It will also be a permanent base for servicing and repairing satellites, which will extend the life of these useful but expensive vessels. All of the necessary tools for reparation will be at the station, which will save the Shuttle a costly trip back to earth with damaged parts.

In addition, the Space Station will allow for the assemblage of oversized structures that are too large for the Orbiter's payload bay—constructions such as huge telescopes, antennae, and experiment platforms. For long-term plans, the space station will provide a stage area for twenty-first-century missions, such as a permanent lunar base, a mission to Mars, a survey of the asteroids, a habitable facility, or a complex of scientific-industrial facilities.

The design of the Space Station has not yet been decided upon, though it's sure to be one that will incorporate minimum risk and maximum station capabilities and will most probably grow out of the preliminary planning program

A docking station for a space colony. The vertical cone-shaped tower contains docking ports where arriving and departing space ships would load and unload. Each spoke contains elevators that connect the hub to the outer ring where the colony's habitat zones are located.

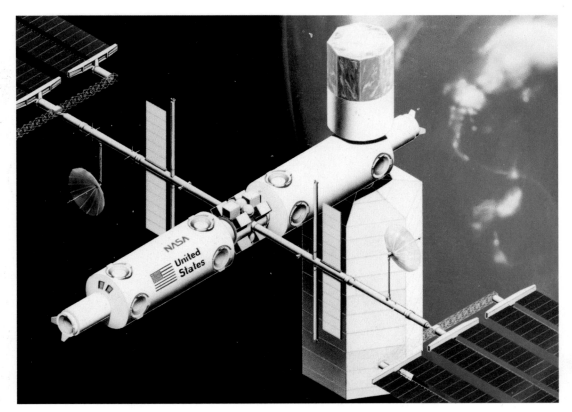

A modular space platform of rotating pallets contains space science and applications payloads with airlocks that join three manned modules. At lower center, the Space Shuttle hovers near a large antenna platform.

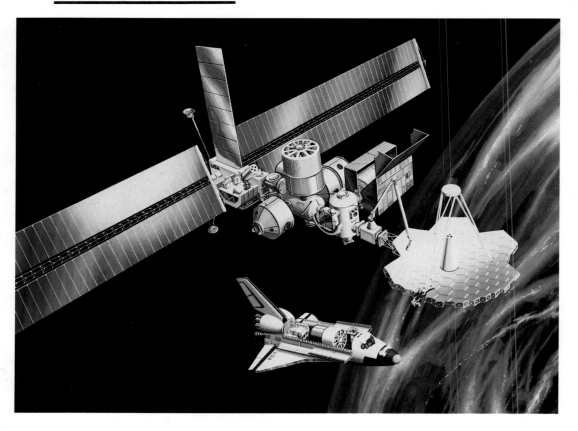

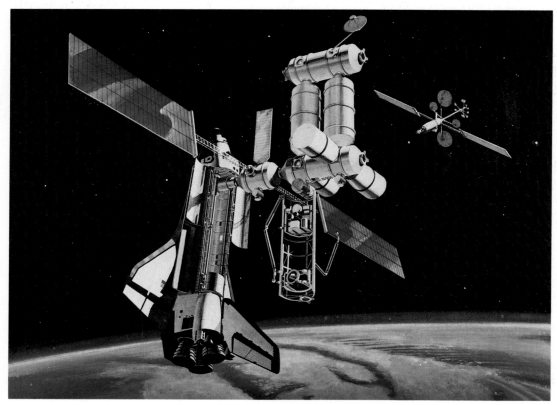

This space station has a base structure consisting of a number of modules clustered with the large wing-like solar panels. The modules provide living quarters for six to eight people, a laboratory and other working areas. The Space Shuttle is shown docked to the Space Station during a mission to resupply the station or to rotate the crew. At the upper right is a communications satellite attached to an orbital transfer vehicle.

In this artist's concept of future lunar operations, a lunar ferry is about to burn out of lunar orbit for the trip back to facilities in low earth orbit. The vehicle carries tank modules filled with liquid oxygen, which has been produced from a mining operation on the surface of the moon. The balloon-like torus around the center of the ferry inflates to several times its illustrated size to take advantage of atmospheric drag to slow and place itself in low earth orbit on its return journey.

NASA has already conducted.

The current concept of the initial Space Station entails two platforms. The first will carry instruments for scientific, technological, and product research and experimentation, and will operate in the same orbit as the main base (yet far enough away to avoid disturbance or contamination) from main-base activities. This platform can be visited by astronauts equipped with maneuvering units for routine inspection. The second platform is still in preliminary planning stages, but it is believed it will be used for manufacturing of pharmaceuticals, alloys, and other substances that are more easily produced in zero gravity.

The central station will have a large solar-power system generating seventy-five kilowatts and each of the platforms will have solar arrays providing twenty-five to thirty-five kilowatts. The manned base will have at least four pressurized modules in which a crew of six to eight will live and work. It will also serve as the docking hub for the Space Shuttle. The Shuttle will be the station's first link to earth, resupplying it and rotating crews at intervals of three to six months.

Of course, at this point the first Space Station is only a plan on an engineer's drawing board, but if we look back to the early days of the space program, almost thirty years ago, we'll recall that a man on the moon was only a dream. With the same courage, dedication, and perseverance, we may one day make this new dream a reality.

AFTERWORD

At the Johnson Space Center in Houston, astronaut trainees take part in zero-gravity training onboard a KC-135 jet. Christa McAuliffe, who was to have been the first teacher in space, is pictured, center. Though training for space travel is serious business, the expressions here show that it can also have its lighter moments. Their optimistic faces show the unflagging spirit that surrounds the space program. Even as America paused to mourn the tragic loss of the Challenger, a "reach for the stars" attitude prevailed.

UPI/BETTMANN NEWSPHOTOS

When President John F. Kennedy challenged NASA to put the first man on the moon by the end of the 1960s, the nation rallied in pursuit of this common goal. On January 28, 1986, the nation once again was united, but this time by a sense of loss of the *Challenger* crew. The flight of the shuttle *Challenger* ended a short seventy-two seconds after lift off. It had reached an altitude of only ten miles. Millions, including school children, watched what was to have been a routine flight (indeed, over twenty successful missions had already been recorded); our successes in space had been so spectacular that a tragedy like this one was unthinkable.

What brought this tragedy even closer to home was the presence on board of America's first teacher in space. If an average citizen could fly in space, then perhaps space travel was no longer a fantastic wonderland for a special few. Dreams of living in space were closer than ever. The immediacy and the significance of the event made the nation mourn the loss of all seven crew

members, Michael J. Smith, Francis R. (Dick) Scobee, Ronald E. McNair, Ellison S. Onizuka, Sharon Christa McAuliffe, Gregory Jarvis, and Judith Resnik, even more acutely.

As a result of the disaster, a stunned nation paused during the days following the accident to reflect on its space program. What we discovered in our grief was that we would not be undone by this tragic temporary setback. The same feelings of national pride that put men on the moon now supported NASA in its conviction to continue with the shuttle program. Punctuating this spirit was the response of the nation's youth. They, perhaps, were most affected by the tragedy; more than just a civilian, Christa McAuliffe was a teacher, someone with whom children could identify on a day-to-day basis. Classes were suspended that day so children all around the nation could watch the first teacher be launched into space. The millions of children (and adults) who watched live as the *Challenger* tumbled back to earth in ashes and flames have an image of the

disaster indelibly printed in their minds. However, children also have a more tremendous investment in the space program—as survival for the future. Encouraged to talk about their reactions to the explosion, children saw the loss, on the whole, as a small part in a much larger scheme, a tragic incident in a mission that should continue.

While this is no happy turn of events, our response to it can be viewed in a more hopeful light, as a testament to America's pioneering spirit. We did pause to ask why and to grieve for our loss, but as we did so, we turned our thoughts to the future. The risks involved in our reach for the stars will not outweigh the unprecedented success we wish to continue there. Space is today's American West, the new frontier; just as the pioneers who lost their lives exploring the middle and western portions of our country would be pleased that we continued the search, so, too, would the last *Challenger* crew want us to pursue the frontier into which they dared to venture.

TIMETABLE OF EVENTS

1958

Oct. 1:	The National Aeronautics and Space Administration is formally inaugurated.
Oct. 7:	NASA approves Project Mercury to send the first American into orbit.
Dec. 18:	Project Score is launched into Earth orbit broadcasting a recorded Christmas message from President Eisenhower.

1959

April 2:	The original seven astronauts are selected for Project Mercury.
Dec. 4:	Monkeynaut "Sam" recovered in Mercury capsule.

1960

April 1:	First meteorological satellite is launched.
May 24:	First experimental infrared surveillance satellite is launched.
Aug. 12:	First experimental passive communications satellite is launched.
Oct. 13:	Three mice—Amy, Sally, and Moe—make successful suborbital flight.
Dec. 19:	First Mercury-Redstone launched (unmanned) into suborbital.

1961

May 5:	Cdr. Alan B. Shepard, Jr., is launched in *Mercury 3* spacecraft *Freedom 7* into a suborbital flight.
July 21:	Lt. Col. Virgil "Gus" Grissom is launched in *Mercury 4* spacecraft *Liberty Bell 7* on suborbital flight.
Nov. 10:	Monkey "Goliath" dies when Atlas rocket is destroyed in flight.
Nov. 29:	*Mercury 5* capsule containing chimpanzee "Enos" is launched.

1962

Feb. 20:	Lt. Col. John Glenn becomes first American to orbit the earth.
May 24:	Lt. Cdr. Scott Carpenter in *Mercury 7* spacecraft *Aurora 7* completes 3 Earth revolutions.
July 10:	NASA launches *Telstar 1,* the first privately owned (AT&T) communications satellite.
Aug. 27:	*Mariner 2* spacecraft is launched. Fly-by probe of Venus is achieved on Dec. 14.
Oct. 3:	Cdr. Walter Schirra, Jr., in *Mercury 8* spacecraft *Sigma 7* completes 6 Earth revolutions.

1963

May 15-16:	Major L. Gordon Cooper, Jr., in Mercury capsule *Faith 7* completes 22 Earth revolutions.

1964

July 28:	NASA launches *Ranger 7* to obtain close-up pictures of the lunar surface.
Aug. 19:	*Syncom 3* communications satellite is launched.
Nov. 28:	*Mariner 4* is on its way to Mars. First fly-by probe completed on July 14, 1965.

1965

Feb. 16: *Pegasus 1* is first vehicle launched with operational payload (meteoroid detector).
June 3-7: Major L. Gordon Cooper, Jr., and Lt. Charles Conrad, Jr., complete 120 Earth revolutions in *Gemini 5.*
Aug. 21-29: Capt. James McDivitt and Capt. Edward White, II, in *Gemini 4* complete 62 Earth revolutions.
Dec. 4-18: Major Frank Borman and Lt.-Cdr. James A. Lovell, Jr., in *Gemini 7* complete 206 Earth revolutions.
Dec. 15-16: Cdr. Walter Schirra and Capt. Thomas Stafford in *Gemini 6* complete 16 Earth revolutions. Mission includes rendezvous and station-keeping with *Gemini 7.*

1966

March 16: Neil A. Armstrong and Capt. David R. Scott in *Gemini 8* complete 6½ Earth revolutions and achieve first docking between a manned spacecraft and an unmanned space vehicle.
May 30: NASA launches *Surveyor 1* to the Moon.
June 3-6: Capt. Thomas Stafford and Lt. Eugene Cernan in *Gemini 9* complete 45 Earth revolutions.
July 18-21: Lt. Cdr. John W. Young and Capt. Michael Collins in *Gemini 10* complete 43 Earth revolutions. First use of target vehicle, *Agena,* as source of propulsion after docking.
Aug. 10: *Lunar Orbiter 1* swings into orbit around the moon.
Sept. 12-15: Lt. Charles Conrad, Jr., and Lt. Cdr. Richard Gordon, Jr., in *Gemini 11* complete 44 Earth revolutions and achieve first rendezvous and docking with target *Agena.*
Nov. 11-15: Lt. Cdr. James Lovell, Jr. and Major Edwin Aldrin, Jr., in *Gemini 12* complete 59 Earth revolutions. Aldrin works outside spacecraft for record 5 hrs. 30 mins.

1967

Jan. 27: Crew of first manned Apollo mission—Lt. Col. Virgil "Gus" Grissom, Lt. Col. Edward H. White, II, and Lt. Cdr. Roger Chaffee—die when a fire breaks out in their command module during a launch pad rehearsal.

1968

Oct. 11-22: Capt. Walter Schirra, Jr., Major Donn Eisele and Walter Cunningham in *Apollo 7* command and service module complete 163 Earth revolutions.
Dec. 21-27: *Apollo 8* orbits the moon ten times with Col. Frank Borman, Capt. James Lovell, Jr., and Lt. Col. William Anders.

1969

Feb. 24: *Mariner 6* launched. Completes fly-by of Mars on July 31.
March 3-13: *Apollo 9* launched into Earth orbit. First flight of complete spacecraft. Onboard: Col. James McDivitt, Col. David Scott, and Russell L. Schweickart.
May 18-26: *Apollo 10* launched for full dress rehearsal of moon landing. On-board: Col. Thomas P. Stafford, Cdr. John W. Young, Cdr. Eugene Cernan.
July 16-24: *Apollo 11* accomplishes the first manned lunar landing. Astronauts Neil A. Armstrong, Lt. Col. Michael Collins and Col. Edwin E. Aldrin, Jr., fulfill goal set by President Kennedy on May 25, 1961 of landing a man on the moon by the end of the decade.
Nov. 14-24: *Apollo 12* launched on second manned lunar landing mission with astronauts Cdr. Charles Conrad, Jr., Cdr. Richard F. Gordon, Jr., Cdr. Alan L. Bean.

1971

July 26–Aug. 7:	*Apollo 15* lunar landing. Astronauts Col. David R. Scott, Lt. Col. James B. Irwin, and Major Alred M. Worden.

1972

Jan. 5:	President Nixon announces approval to develop Space Shuttle.
March 3:	*Pioneer 10* is launched on 21-month fly-by mission to Jupiter.
April 16–27:	NASA launches *Apollo 16* on sixth lunar landing mission. Astronauts Capt. John W. Young, Cdr. Thomas K. Mattingly, II, and Col. Charles M. Duke.
July 23:	NASA launches first Earth Resources Technology Satellite (ERTS-1) later renamed *Landsat 1.*
Dec. 7–19:	Apollo 17—last lunar landing mission. Astronauts Capt. Eugene A. Cernan, Lt. Cdr. Ronald E. Evans and Dr. Harrison Schmitt.

1973

April 16:	*Pioneer 11* launched on fly-by mission to Jupiter and Saturn.
May 14:	*Skylab 1* space station launched into Earth orbit.
May 25–June 22:	*Skylab 2* ferry with astronauts Capt. Charles Conrad, Jr., Dr. Joseph Kerwin and Capt. Paul Weitz is launched.
July 28–Sept. 25:	*Skylab 3* ferry with astronauts Capt. Alan Bean, Major Jack Lousma and Dr. Owen Garriott is launched.
Nov. 3:	*Mariner 10* is launched on a double-planet mission to Venus (February 5, 1974) and to Mercury (March 29, 1974).
Nov. 16–Feb. 8:	*Skylab 4* ferry with astronauts Lt. Col. Gerald P. Carr, Dr. Edward Gibson, and Lt. Col. William Pogue.

1975

July 17:	Apollo joined the Soviet Soyuz in orbit 140 miles (224 km.) above Earth.
Aug. 20:	*Viking 1* spacecraft to Mars is launched.
Sept. 9:	NASA launches *Viking 2* spacecraft to Mars.

1976

Feb. 10:	*Pioneer 10* crosses Saturn's orbit on its way out of the Solar System.
March 17:	NASA announces four crews for the first flights of the Space Shuttle: Fred Haise, Jr., Lt. Col. Charles Fullerton; Col. Joe Engle, Cdr. Richard Truly; Capt. John Young, Cdr. Robert Crippen; and Lt. Col. Jack Lousma and Vance Brand.

1977

Aug. 12:	Space Shuttle Orbiter *Enterprise* with astronauts Fred Haise, Jr., and Lt. Col. Charles Fullerton makes first free flight from Boeing *747.*
Aug. 20:	*Voyager 2* launched on multiplanet fly-by mission to Jupiter (July 1979), Saturn (August 1981) and possibly Uranus (January 1986) and Neptune (1989).
Sept. 5:	*Voyager 1* launched on fly-by mission to Jupiter (March 1979) and Saturn (Nov. 1980).
Sept. 13:	Space Shuttle Orbiter *Enterprise* flown by Col. Joe Engle and Cdr. Richard Truly makes second free flight from back of Boeing of *747.*

Sept. 23: Space Shuttle Orbiter *Enterprise,* flown by Fred Haise and Lt. Charles Fullerton makes third free flight from Boeing *747.*

Oct. 12 Space Shuttle Orbiter *Enterprise* with astronauts Col. Joe Engle and Cdr. Richard Truly make fourth free flight from Boeing *747.*

Oct. 26: Space Shuttle Orbiter *Enterprise* makes fifth and last flight from Boeing *747* with astronauts Haise and Fullerton.

1978

May 20: *Pioneer-Venus 1* is launched; it swings into orbit around Venus on December 4.

Aug. 8: NASA launches *Pioneer-Venus 2.*

1979

March 5: *Voyager 1* flies within 177,720 miles (284,352 km.) of Jupiter's clouds, giving us startling new information.

May 1: Space Shuttle *Enterprise* is rolled out of the Vehicle Assembly Building for its first solo flight.

July 9: *Voyager 2* flies within 399,560 miles (639,296 km.) of Jupiter's clouds.

Sept. 1: *Pioneer 11* flies within 13,000 miles (20,800 km.) of Saturn's clouds.

1980

Nov. 12: *Voyager 1* flies within 77,000 miles (123,200 km.) of Saturn's cloud tops making detailed studies of the planet, its spectacular ring system and various moons.

1981

April 12–14: First orbital test flight of Space Shuttle *Columbia* with John W. Young as commander and Capt. Robert L. Crippen as pilot.

Aug. 25: *Voyager 2* passes within 63,000 miles (100,800 km.) of the cloud tops of Saturn.

Nov. 12–14: Second orbital test flight of Space Shuttle *Columbia.*

1982

January: NASA announces that data supplied by *Voyager 2* during close encounter with Saturn in August 1981 led to discovery of four more moons.

March 22–30: Third orbital test flight of Space Shuttle *Columbia.*

June 27–July 4: Fourth and final test flight of Space Shuttle *Columbia.*

July 16: NASA launches 4,273 lb. (1,593.83 kg.) Earth Resources Satellite *Landsat 4* into Sun-synchronous orbit.

Sept. 29: NASA announces agreement to train Canadians for Space Shuttle mission specialists.

Nov. 11–16: Space Shuttle *Columbia* makes fifth flight into orbit.

Dec. 22: NASA announces agreement to have Australians trained as Space Shuttle mission specialists.

1983

Jan. 25: NASA launches infrared astronomical satellite.

April 4–9: Space Shuttle *Challenger*'s maiden flight with Commander Paul Weitz, pilot Colonel Karol Bobko, Mission Specialist Dr. Storey Musgrave and Donald Peterson.

TIMETABLE OF EVENTS

June 13:   *Pioneer 10* crosses orbit of Neptune at 30,552 miles (48,883.2 km.) per hour on its way out of the solar system.

June 18–24:   Space Shuttle *Challenger* is launched for the second time with Capt. Robert Crippen (commander), Cdr. Frederick Hauck (pilot), and Mission Specialists Lt. Col. John Fabian, Dr. Sally K. Ride (first American woman in space), and Dr. Norman Thagard.

Aug. 30–Sept. 6:   NASA launches *Challenger* STS-8 with Captain Richard Truly (commander), Cdr. Daniel Brandenstein (pilot), and three mission specialists: Lt. Cdr. Dale Gardner, Lt. Col. Guion Bluford, and Dr. William Thornton. Bluford is the first black American astronaut.

Oct. 24:   NASA names the Space Shuttle telescope (to be launched in 1986) after Edwin P. Hubble, one of America's leading astronomers.

Nov. 28–Dec. 8:   Space Shuttle *Columbia* launched. Initial flight of the Spacelab orbital laboratory.

1984

Feb. 3–11:   Space Shuttle *Challenger* launched. Mission Specialist Bruce McCandless, II, makes maiden voyage to orbit wearing a Manned Maneuvering Unit (MMU).

Aug. 27:   President Reagan announces that the first citizen passenger in orbit should be an educator. NASA is accepting applications.

The first flight of the Space Shuttle *Discovery.*

1985

July: The first made-in-space product, polystyrene beads, are available on the commercial market.

July 12:   *Spacelab 2* lifts off.

July 19:   Christa McAuliffe is chosen by NASA to be the first "average citizen" to go into space.

1986

Jan. 28:   *Challenger* explodes 72 seconds after lift off killing all seven crew members including America's first teacher in space, Christa McAuliffe. This marks NASA's first human fatalities during a mission.

FURTHER READING

Space Vehicles

American Institute of Aeronautics and Astronautics. *Space Transportation Systems: 1980-2000.* New York: American Institute of Aeronautics and Astronautics, 1979.

Baker, David. *The Rocket: The History and Development of Rocket and Missile Technology.* New York: Crown, 1978.

Murphy, Lynn C. *Rockets, Missiles, and Spacecraft of the National Air and Space Museum.* Washington, D.C.: Smithsonian Institution Press, 1976.

Powers, Robert M. *Shuttle: The World's First Spaceship.* Harrisburg, PA: Stackpole Books, 1979.

Von Braun, Wernher, and Frederick I. Ordway III. *History of Rocketry and Space Travel.* New York: Crowell, 1975.

The Earth From Outside

Diagram Group. *Spaceship Earth: Its Voyage Through Time.* New York: Hearst Books, 1980.

Dickson, Paul. *Out of This World: American Space Photography.* New York: Delacourte, 1977.

Francis, Peter and Pat Jones. *Images of Earth.* Englewood Cliffs, NJ: Prentice-Hall, 1984.

Lowman, Paul D., Jr. *The Third Planet: Terrestrial Geology in Orbital Photographs.* Charlottesville, VA: University of Virginia Press: 1972.

United States National Aeronautics and Space Administration. *High Altitude Perspective.* Washington, D.C.: NASA, Government Printing Office, 1978.

Planets of the Solar System

Briggs, Geoffrey and Fredric Taylor. *The Cambridge Photographic Atlas of the Planets.* Cambridge: Cambridge University Press, 1982.

Burgess, Eric. *To the Red Planet.* New York: Columbia University Press, 1978.

Chapman, Clark R. *Inner Planets: New Light on the Rocky Worlds of Mercury, Venus, Earth, the Moon, Mars and the Asteroids.* New York: Scribners, 1977.

Corliss, William R. *Mysterious Universe: A Handbook of Astronomical Anomalies.* Glen Arms, MD: The Sourcebook Project, 1979.

Eddy, John A. *A New Sun: The Solar Results from Skylab.* Washington, D.C.: NASA, Government Printing Office, 1979.

Moore, Patrick. *New Concise Atlas of the Universe.* Chicago: Rand McNally, 1978.

Tombaugh, Clyde W. and Patrick Moore. *Out of the Darkness: The Planet Pluto.* London: Lutterworth Press, 1980.

Von Braun, Wernher and Frederick I. Ordway III. *New Worlds: Discoveries from Our Solar System.* New York: Doubleday, 1979.

The Stars and Planets Beyond

Edelson, Edward. *Who Goes There? The Search for Intelligent Life in the Universe.* New York: Doubleday, 1979.

Ferris, Timothy. *Galaxies.* New York: Scribners, 1980.

Friedlander, Michael W. *Astronomy: From Stonehenge to Quasars.* Englewood Cliffs, NJ: Prentice-Hall, 1985.

Mitton, Simon. *Exploring the Galaxies.* New York: Scribners, 1977.

Ridpath, Ian. *Messages from the Stars.* New York: Harper & Row, 1978.

People in Space

Aldrin, Col. Edwin E. with Wayne Varga. *Return to Earth.* New York: Random House, 1973.

Allen, Joseph P. and Russell Martin. *Entering Space.* New York: Stewart, Tabori & Chang, 1984.

Collins, Michael. *Carrying the Fire: An Astronaut's Journeys.* New York: Farrar, Straus & Giroux: 1974.

Cunningham, Walter. *The All-American Boys.* New York: Macmillan, 1977.

Irwin, James B. with William A. Emerson, Jr. *To Rule the Night: The Discovery Voyage of Astronaut Jim Irwin.* Nashville, TN: Holman Co., 1973.

Segel, Thomas D. *Men in Space.* Boulder, CO: Sycamore Island Books, 1975.

Wolfe, Tom. *The Right Stuff.* New York: Farrar, Straus & Giroux, 1979.

Space Equipment

Gatland, Kenneth. *The Illustrated Encyclopedia of Space Technology.* New York: Harmony Books, 1981.

Spacelab 2. Washington, D.C.: NASA, Government Printing Office, 1985.

The Future in Space

Adelman, Saul J. and Benjamin Adelman. *Bound for the Stars.* Englewood Cliffs, NJ: Prentice-Hall, 1980.

Billingham, John, William Gilbreath, and Brian O'Leary, eds. *Space Resources and Space Settlements.* Washington, D.C.: NASA, Government Printing Office, 1979.

Brand, Stewart, ed. *Space Colonies.* New York: Co-Evolution Quarterly (Penguin Books), 1977.

Freeman, Michael. *Space Traveller's Handbook: Everyman's Comprehensive Manual to Space Flight.* New York: Sovereign Books (Simon & Schuster), 1979.

O'Neill, Gerard K. *The High Frontier: Human Colonies in Space.* New York: William Morrow, 1977.

Stine, G. Harry. *The Third Industrial Revolution.* New York: Putnam, 1975.

Tanner, Dan and George Johnson. *Cities in Space.* Eugene, OR: Harvest House, 1979.

INDEX